Especially for

....

From

....

Date

....

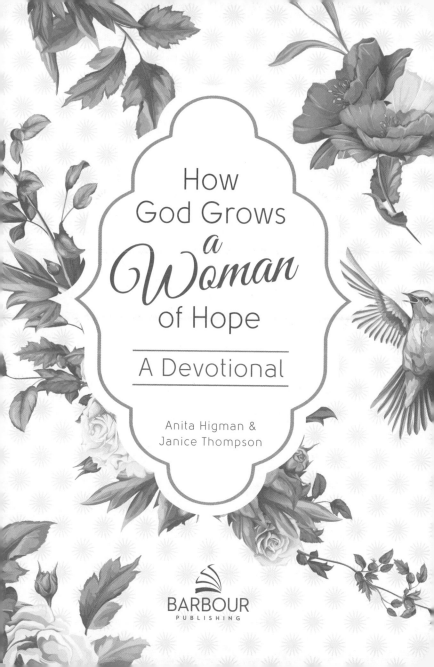

How
God Grows
a *Woman*
of Hope

A Devotional

Anita Higman &
Janice Thompson

BARBOUR
PUBLISHING

© 2021 by Barbour Publishing, Inc.

Print ISBN 978-1-64352-701-7

Published by Barbour Publishing, Inc., 1810 Barbour Drive, Uhrichsville, Ohio 44683, www.barbourbooks.com

Our mission is to inspire the world with the life-changing message of the Bible.

Member of the
Evangelical Christian
Publishers Association

Printed in China.

I dedicate this book to the Lord Jesus Christ,
who has given me every kind of wonderful gift—
art, music, nature, family, friends, and love.
But above all—through Christ's
sacrifice and resurrection—
He has given me the gift of hope!

Anita Higman

To my nine grandchildren.
You bring me such hope for the future!

Janice Thompson

Introduction

Life can be a jumbled assortment of pretty things and ugly things. On the ugly days, we may struggle with an overwhelming sense of hopelessness. But appearances can be deceiving, because we don't see into the supernatural world and all that God is busy doing on our behalf. We may not always know what is coming or how all our troubles will be resolved, but we have every reason to believe this world is still in the mighty hands of the One who created it, the One who offers us redemption in Christ, and the One who tenderly woos us, changes us, and lovingly sustains us every day, every hour, and with every breath.

May these devotional offerings bring you to that soul-awakening place of hope!

Oh, to Be
Known by You!

"What's the price of a pet canary? Some loose change, right?
And God cares what happens to it even more than you do.
He pays even greater attention to you, down to the last detail—
even numbering the hairs on your head! So don't be intimidated
by all this bully talk. You're worth more than a million canaries."
MATTHEW 10:29–31 MSG

Falling in love is unlike any other experience on earth. It is, well, *lovely*! Couples falling in love try to get to know everything about each other—every little detail. It is simply part of that achingly beautiful "falling" part. Love is so glorious, so full of life and hope! And like a man and woman getting to know each other, the Lord knows each of us very well indeed. God might say something like, "You are My beloved, whom I delight in. I know you love hiking through the forests and finding little woodland surprises like miniature owls or maidenhair ferns or gurgling brooks. I know you enjoy vanilla gelato. And you always, always cry when you hear the song "Danny Boy." You or I might then reply, "I love You too, God. Here's a list of all the things I love about You. . . ."

To be known by You, Lord, is the loveliest thing. You even
know the number of hairs on my head! Have I told You today
all the wondrous things I love about You? Amen. —AH

Better Than New Gloves

John the Baptist: The person who has two shirts must share with the person who has none. And the person with food must share with the one in need.

LUKE 3:11 VOICE

Juliet had a great time at the mall, shopping for new gloves. She'd purchased some soft leather ones. And when she slipped them on—oh my. Cozy, creamy bliss.

Then Juliet dropped by her local food pantry on the way home to donate some sacks of canned goods that she'd picked up earlier in the day. She hadn't thought much about the donation, but the ladies at the pantry were almost teary-eyed with gratefulness when she came in with so many supplies. You see, the need had been great during the holidays, and their shelves had nearly gone empty. Both of the female volunteers hugged Juliet, thanking her multiple times for her kindness and generosity.

As Juliet was driving home, her eyes stung with joyful tears. The gloves and the donation had cost about the same amount of money. Even though Juliet still thought shopping was fun, she had to admit that the hugs and words of gratitude from those volunteers did far more to warm and delight her spirit than the finest gloves on earth.

Juliet's deed not only brought hope to the needy and pleased the Lord, but the gift uplifted her needy heart as well.

Oh Lord, help me to be generous with others, for I know my generosity brings You delight. Amen. —AH

To Give You Hope

"For I know the plans I have for you," declares the LORD,
"plans to prosper you and not to harm you,
plans to give you hope and a future."
JEREMIAH 29:11 NIV

The long snow-laden winter had Ashley worn down to a tired and dreary mess of emotions. The trees had all gone bald, there was little sunshine to speak of, and when the wind blew it felt like she'd been transported to a howling wilderness! Then one morning in her back-yard Ashley spotted a tendril of life in her flower bed, a delicate stem curling upward and unfurling into a bright blossom. What pray tell was that? It was a flower Ashley had never planted, yet there it was, head held up and blooming its little heart out. It was a tiny miracle in the snow. Yes, what hope she felt seeing such unexpected life and color—not to mention the promise of spring to come.

If God has plans and promises for the flowers in the winter, He surely has plans and promises for you. Even in the bleakest of winters, may we be sustained by His hope and the promise of spring.

Lord, in those dark days of winter, please fill me with
Your life and hope. I need You every day and in
every season of my life! Amen. —AH

Glimpses of Heaven

Eternal One: Now look here! I am creating new heavens
and a new earth. The weary and painful past will be as if it never
happened. No one will talk or even think about it anymore.
Isaiah 65:17 voice

The woman was at her wits' end. Her friends had abandoned her. Her family didn't call or drop by anymore. And the evening news and social media were getting darker by the day. Then the woman happened to see an online photo of a fairy-tale house. The outside was decorated ornately and the arched front door was festooned with hundreds of pink roses. The whimsical cottage looked so warm and welcoming and wonderful that the woman burst into tears. She wondered why something so exquisite would cause such an emotional stir. She sat quietly to think on it, and then she realized what had happened. The sheer beauty of the scene reminded her that humankind was still capable of beauty—that humans still showed hints of God's original divine imprint on them. That we could still get glimmers of paradise, and when we do see them, the view breaks through our defenses—for deep down we search for all that is beautiful and lovely and good. In other words, our souls long for God.

The woman wept some more, and this time, they were tears of joy and hope.

Thank You, Lord, for hope-filled glimpses
of Your kingdom that is to come! Amen. —AH

Even Better Than Cake!

*If we claim we have not sinned, we are calling God a liar
and showing that his word has no place in our hearts.*
1 JOHN 1:10 NLT

People don't apologize much anymore. Why? For one thing, the thought of having to apologize makes us squirm. It seems like a lot more fun to go eat a big slice of chocolate cake than to go to a friend and say, "You know what? I see that I have hurt you. I was wrong in doing that. I'm sorry, and I'll try not to do it again in the future. Will you forgive me?" No, those words don't come easily to humans. But we are called to humility, and humility means admitting that we've messed up and asking for forgiveness.

God wants us to grow to be like Him, but He loves us the way we are and shows us forbearance and compassion in working with us as we grow in Him. And of course He would love for us to show others the same benevolence of spirit. Oh, what hope there is in the freeing feeling of forgiving and being forgiven. Even better than eating cake!

*Heavenly Father, thank You for Your mercy and patience
with me as I grow in my faith. May I generously offer
forgiveness to others as You have so generously offered
it to me. In Jesus' holy name I pray. Amen. —AH*

Our Only Hope

*But blessed is the man who trusts in the Lord
and has made the Lord his hope and confidence.*

JEREMIAH 17:7 TLB

After much rocking and tugging, the rope that kept the little boat secured to the dock eventually came untethered. No one paid any attention to the vessel as it bobbed and drifted ever so slowly away from its safe harbor inside the quiet inlet cove and into the deep waters of the lake. After a while, a storm rose up, and some serious winds and waves made the vessel dip and pitch like it was a mere toy. With no one in sight to bring it home, the little craft was in danger of slamming against the rocks and capsizing.

Sometimes when we're not paying attention, we too can come untethered spiritually as we give in to temptation and sin. Even as Christians, we can get ourselves into some serious trouble. Fortunately, we always have Someone to bring us home. Always. May we put our trust in the Lord Jesus. May we seek His lavish forgiveness and His loving presence. May we cling to the One who is our greatest hope.

*Dear God, I choose to trust in You always.
Thank You for the hope You've given me in Christ Jesus.
I am eternally grateful to You! Amen. —AH*

He Will Quiet You

"The Lᴏʀᴅ your God is in your midst, a mighty one who will save;
he will rejoice over you with gladness; he will quiet you by
his love; he will exult over you with loud singing."
Zᴇᴘʜᴀɴɪᴀʜ 3:17 ᴇsᴠ

This earth may seem like a pretty blue and green sphere spinning silently and peacefully in outer space, but on closer inspection—when you get up close and personal on the streets and in the hearts of mankind—this world is anything but quiet and peace filled. It can be a clamoring and dangerous place to live. Noise and chaos spew from all our devices—which too easily become vices—morning, noon, and night. There doesn't seem to be any escape from every kind of anxiety, whether the cause is imagined or real.

So what can be done about it? Simply put, we need less TV, phone, and social media time—and more God time.

More God time means healing for the body, mind, and soul. More God time means refreshment and delight. More God time equals hope.

Father God, show me how to unplug from all the clamor
around me and plug into a life with You by my side. Lead me near
green meadows and soothing waters, and may my anxious soul
be quieted by Your love. In Jesus' name I pray. Amen. —AH

The Gospel Needs No Makeover

*I am astonished that you are so quickly deserting the one
who called you to live in the grace of Christ and are turning
to a different gospel—which is really no gospel at all.
Evidently some people are throwing you into confusion and
are trying to pervert the gospel of Christ. But even if we or
an angel from heaven should preach a gospel other than the
one we preached to you, let them be under God's curse!*

GALATIANS 1:6–8 NIV

Makeovers have become so popular. I mean, who doesn't want to see a woman go from frump to fab? Who doesn't want to see an old barn made into a breathtaking chateau? But one thing that should never, ever be refurbished is the Gospel of Christ. Christians need to be on guard against and ever watchful for Satan's ploys. We need to beware of anyone who adds to or alters or creatively "refreshes" the basic Gospel message, thus leading us away from Christ. May it never be!

Okay, so how can we know if a different gospel is being promoted in books or on TV or social media? We will know by reading the Word of God, spending time in prayer, and fellowshipping within the body of believers. The Gospel is not a secret. Nor is it meant to be complicated or confusing. It is truth and freedom. It is the hope that will satisfy like nothing else!

*Lord Jesus, may I never be led astray
by a different gospel. Amen. —AH*

Blushing 101

They acted shamefully, they committed abomination; yet they were not at all ashamed, they did not know how to blush. Therefore they shall fall among those who fall; at the time when I punish them, they shall be overthrown, says the LORD.

JEREMIAH 8:12 NRSV

The young man stumbled around in the conversation until the young woman he was with suddenly blushed. The man realized he'd said something kind of "off" or perhaps even offensive, so he humbly apologized. This scenario seems more and more farfetched in today's society. People don't blush easily anymore. They may not feel all that remorseful over their blunders or sins. Meekness and righteousness seem to be considered weaknesses these days.

Now why is that?

Perhaps we have seen too much. Over the decades we have become anesthetized to all kinds of sights and behaviors. What was once considered an abomination to God is now tolerated and even celebrated. We have been made to feel that innocence is nonsense and that keeping it edgy is keeping it real. Perhaps we have been tempted to become the world as we live in the world. But once we are truly a part of the world, what do we have to witness about? What hope can we share?

Dearest Lord, help me to be a woman who is guileless, virtuous, and humble. Amen. —AH

17

What We Crave

God's readiness to give and forgive is now public. Salvation's available for everyone! We're being shown how to turn our backs on a godless, indulgent life, and how to take on a God-filled, God-honoring life. This new life is starting right now, and is whetting our appetites for the glorious day when our great God and Savior, Jesus Christ, appears. He offered himself as a sacrifice to free us from a dark, rebellious life into this good, pure life, making us a people he can be proud of, energetic in goodness.

TITUS 2:11–14 MSG

Most folks have never heard of people craving substances such as pebbles, metal, hair, paint, chalk, and paper. But it does happen. It's a psychological disorder called pica. Hard to imagine embracing such a bizarre snacking habit—one that could kill a person!

But *spiritually* speaking, we may be choosing to do something similar to that every day. Anytime we partake of what is on the world's buffet—of self-indulgent desires and ungodliness—we cannot thrive. It will become as hazardous and horrible as dining on rocks! May each of our souls gain an appetite for what will nourish and heal us. What will make us grow and thrive. What will bring us life and hope.

Holy Spirit, teach me how to live in the world but not be a part of it. Help me to grow into a godly woman of love, beauty, and hope. Amen. —AH

That Perfect Moment in Time

*God will wipe away every tear from their eyes; and death
shall be no more, neither shall there be anguish (sorrow
and mourning) nor grief nor pain any more, for the old
conditions and the former order of things have passed away.*
REVELATION 21:4 AMPC

Your little baby loves bath time, right? And so you ever so gingerly place her in the miniature tub. She splashes and wiggles in the warm water and coos and grins at you with such trust and innocence and love that a joyful mist stings your eyes. Before you know it, your heart has melted into an intoxicating pool of baby love.

But even that blissful and near-perfect moment on earth will never be able to come close to one moment—any moment at all—in heaven. Why? Because we will be in the presence of pure light and beauty and love—God. We will have knowledge and purpose and wisdom, joy and delight and creativity beyond anything we can imagine here. We will no longer feel petty or superficial or hurt. No more disappointments, or loneliness, or unfulfilled dreams. Fear and pain and death will be no more. If there are tears, they will be ones of joy. Ah, such glorious hope!

*Lord Jesus, thank You for Your redemption and
the hope of heaven. How thrilling it is! Amen. —AH*

A Hope-Filled Place

*They heard the sound of the LORD God walking in the
garden at the time of the evening breeze, and the
man and his wife hid themselves from the presence
of the LORD God among the trees of the garden.*

GENESIS 3:8 NRSV

Adam and Eve lived a life of wonder and love and joy and purpose, and they had every glorious thing imaginable available to them. And yet Adam and Eve demanded more. They didn't just want to walk with God; they wanted to *be* God Almighty! Talk about ungrateful, not to mention rebellious and arrogant. Imagine!

And yet every time we step away from Christ, even for a moment, we are romancing a similar notion in our spirits and in essence saying: "Lord, I don't need You right now. I've got this one."

Here's what we should be saying, "Walk with me, Lord, in the cool of the evening. And in every moment of every day. I can't do any of life without You. I can't even breathe without You! There is no more peaceful or joyful or hope-filled place to be than in Your sweet presence!"

---

*Lord Jesus, please be ever near me.
You mean everything to me, both now
and forevermore! Amen. —AH*

Where Real Hope Resides

Jesus answered, "My kingdom is not of this world.
If my kingdom were of this world, my servants would
have been fighting, that I might not be delivered over
to the Jews. But my kingdom is not from the world."
JOHN 18:36 ESV

The Jews—including the disciples—hoped that Jesus would eventually topple Roman rule and reign on earth. But we should be profoundly grateful that the Lord didn't fulfill that wish of mankind. That kind of earthly revolt and triumph over the government in Jesus' day would have been only a temporary fix to a deeply rooted problem as old as Eden. People can be shortsighted because they can't see their lives in the light of eternity. God sees from a very different vantage point—one that illuminates time without end.

Jesus came for a revolution, yes, but one concerning the soul—a revolt against sin and death.

And if we have become followers of Christ, we are to be emissaries of His love to the world. May we share the hope of salvation with this broken and needy world!

Lord, I know why You came to earth, and I am eternally
grateful for Your mercy and grace. Please show me
how to share Your Good News of hope! Amen. —AH

Welcome to the Light!

*When Jesus spoke again to the people, he said,
"I am the light of the world. Whoever follows me will
never walk in darkness, but will have the light of life."*
JOHN 8:12 NIV

Ava proceeded cautiously out of the cave—where she had been taking an extended tour—and stepped out into the brilliant noonday sun. She appreciated the light but held her hand over her eyes, since the light was brighter than she remembered only an hour before. Her eyes had gotten used to the darkness, so she needed time to readjust.

It's easy to get used to darkness. The enemy of our souls knows very well just how easy it is.

In the Gospel of John we read, "Then Jesus told them, 'You are going to have the light just a little while longer. Walk while you have the light, before darkness overtakes you. Whoever walks in the dark does not know where they are going. Believe in the light while you have the light, so that you may become children of light.' When he had finished speaking, Jesus left and hid himself from them" (12:35–36 NIV).

As Christians, when we walk into a room, may people see the radiant light and hope we have in Christ!

*Jesus, help me to reflect Your holy light
in this dark and hurting world. Amen. —AH*

Each Word a Gift

*And let us consider how to stir up one another to love
and good works, not neglecting to meet together,
as is the habit of some, but encouraging one another,
and all the more as you see the Day drawing near.*
HEBREWS 10:24–25 ESV

Peggy felt dog-tired from all the volunteer work she'd done at church. It had been a hard few months, and she was running on fumes. Fellow parishioners hadn't been all that helpful as she tried to revive the women's ministry. Mostly, the people around her tended to poke at her rather than praise her for all her efforts. Finally, one morning, as Peggy was arranging the daisies on one of the tables for a community outreach luncheon, someone strolled by and flippantly told her the table flowers looked a bit wilted. That was the last straw. Peggy found an empty restroom and cried her heart out. Poor Peggy. She had given it her all, and no one had been there to encourage her along the way.

In Ephesians, the apostle Paul reminds us, "Watch the way you talk. Let nothing foul or dirty come out of your mouth. Say only what helps, each word a gift" (4:29 MSG).

As lovers of Christ, may we think of our words as gifts, and may those gifts be ones of hope, love, and encouragement!

Lord, help me to be an encourager! Amen. —AH

What Glorious Hope

But his joy is in those who reverence him,
those who expect him to be loving and kind.
<small>PSALM 147:11 TLB</small>

Little Bella stuck out her lower lip in hopes her parents wouldn't be too hard on her for accidentally breaking a living room vase. But deep down Bella wasn't too worried, since she knew her parents were loving and kind and fair. And sure enough, Bella was right. After she explained what had happened to the vase and how sorry she was, her parents forgave her, offered some suggestions for the future, and then helped her clean up the mess. Bella sighed with relief as she snuggled into their hugs. Oh, how she loved her parents.

How do we see our Lord? Do we see Him as a parent who loves us so much that we expect Him to be loving and kind and fair? Do we go to Him when we think we have failed in some way? Do we expect forgiveness and fairness and His loving arms around us?

What glorious hope there is in God's love. It makes us want to smile and shout and sigh in joy.

Thank You, Lord, that I can come to You no
matter what I've done. I am confident of
Your love and kindness! Amen. —AH

Every Reason to Hope

In the same way, we can see and understand only a little about God now, as if we were peering at his reflection in a poor mirror; but someday we are going to see him in his completeness, face-to-face. Now all that I know is hazy and blurred, but then I will see everything clearly, just as clearly as God sees into my heart right now. There are three things that remain—faith, hope, and love—and the greatest of these is love.

1 CORINTHIANS 13:12–13 TLB

Iris cleaned the antique mirror, but still it remained hazy. Well, it was an antique after all. But even then, something in her wanted the mirror to be clear. The haze seemed annoying and cheerless. Iris finally gave up and placed the old mirror in a back room.

Perhaps we have a similar desire when it comes to seeing God. We want to see Him, know Him, but no matter how hard we try, on this side of eternity, we will see only dimly.

Oh, but one day we will see the Lord face-to-face. No more haziness or blurred vision. We will see God in His completeness, and we will be filled with more joy than we thought our hearts could ever hold. What hope is yet to come!

*Praise You, Lord Jesus, for faith,
hope, and love! Amen. —AH*

Back to God's Word

The whole Bible was given to us by inspiration
from God and is useful to teach us what is true
and to make us realize what is wrong in our lives;
it straightens us out and helps us do what is right.

2 TIMOTHY 3:16 TLB

Have you ever stumbled so badly in your Christian walk that you wanted to remark about your life, "I guess no fools need apply. I've already got the job!"

You are not alone in your foolhardy mess. Even the biblical hero King David slipped and stumbled, but God loved him dearly and kept working with him all through his life. So we can take heart and know that no matter how badly we've stumbled, God still loves us dearly. He wants to keep working with us, helping us, and loving us right into heaven.

One way to let God work with us is to get more serious about reading and studying God's Living Word. This one-of-a-kind Book will inspire us, change us, teach us, challenge us, and encourage us. The Bible will straighten us out and help us to live right!

Dearest Lord Jesus, help me to dig into Your
Holy Word with gusto. Not out of obligation
but out of a fervent love for You! Amen. —AH

God Got Personal

So with us; while we were minors, we were enslaved to the elemental spirits of the world. But when the fullness of time had come, God sent his Son, born of a woman, born under the law, in order to redeem those who were under the law, so that we might receive adoption as children.

GALATIANS 4:3–5 NRSV

God could have come up with a thousand different ways to redeem mankind, but He chose to get personal. He chose not to be a standoffish kind of father. He is so profoundly intimate and loving, in fact, that His Son, Jesus, took on the confinement of growing in a womb, the vulnerability of being raised by a teenage mother, and the messiness of growing up amid the general chaos of siblings! Jesus wasn't born in a palace. He didn't know an upbringing with lavish surroundings or an entourage of encouragers. Instead, Jesus came as a servant, knowing great suffering and abandonment and death. And amazingly—almost unbelievably—He did it all for us.

May we embrace the Lord's grace and His up-close-and-personal way of loving us. How about you? Have you gotten personal with God?

I praise You, Jesus, for coming to save me in such a unique and humble and profound way. Your sacrifice has made all the difference in my life! Amen. —AH

Thankfulness

And as they entered a village there, ten lepers stood at a distance, crying out, "Jesus, sir, have mercy on us!" He looked at them and said, "Go to the Jewish priest and show him that you are healed!" And as they were going, their leprosy disappeared. One of them came back to Jesus, shouting, "Glory to God, I'm healed!" He fell flat on the ground in front of Jesus, face downward in the dust, thanking him for what he had done. This man was a despised Samaritan. Jesus asked, "Didn't I heal ten men? Where are the nine? Does only this foreigner return to give glory to God?"

LUKE 17:12–18 TLB

How many times have we left a party or a lunch at someone's house only to realize that we forgot to thank the hostess? Or we forgot to thank a friend for her gracious gift or prayer or kindness. Forgetting to be considerate happens all the time. To everyone. We are a busy people. But expressing gratitude is a beautiful thing.

Look how it worked out for that one man in ancient times who remembered to go back and thank Jesus for his healing. The former leper was able to spend a few more precious moments with the Savior. He pleased the Lord with his grateful attitude. And he got an important mention in the most important book on earth—the Bible.

May we all be thankful to others and, most importantly, to our God!

*Lord, may I never be too busy
to be thankful! Amen. —AH*

May We Rustle with Praise!

Let the heavens be glad, the earth rejoice; let the
vastness of the roaring seas demonstrate his glory.
Praise him for the growing fields, for they display his
greatness. Let the trees of the forest rustle with praise.
PSALM 96:11–12 TLB

Every day, things happen to us that have the potential to weigh us down spiritually. Maybe we have a hard time getting out of bed, let alone rustling with praise like the trees of the forest! We might end up enduring disappointments, loss, accidents, bad news, snubs, our own transgressions, natural disasters, betrayals, misunderstandings, and a host of other "earth weights."

And yet even in the midst of this heaviness of spirit, we can take a tip from nature and continue to demonstrate God's glory. Impossible? It will feel that way at times. But there is no place better to be than near to the heart of God. Cry out to Him. The Lord has the supernatural strength and endless mercy and divine love and sweet hope not only to pull you through these troubles but to help you rustle with praise!

Mighty God, when the heaviness of earth gets to me,
be near me and help me to display Your greatness even in
the middle of these trials. In Jesus' name I pray. Amen. —AH

A Different Life

Am I now seeking human approval, or God's approval?
Or am I trying to please people? If I were still pleasing
people, I would not be a servant of Christ.

GALATIANS 1:10 NRSV

The poor dear woman tried to please all the people around her, but somehow it rarely worked. She'd grown up not knowing the cheering support of her parents, so to make up for it, she found herself trapped, ever spinning her wheels, trying to gain the applause of anyone and everyone. On her fortieth birthday she woke up in a wild panic, thinking she was headed for a nervous breakdown.

Right then, the woman knelt by her bed and poured out her heart to the only Person she could really trust with her panic and pain—Jesus. She told Him of her history, even though He already knew it well. She told the Lord of how she finally had to let go of her endless striving. She simply could not dance any faster or jump any higher. She surrendered it all right there. After some joyful tears and a cup of tea, she wondered why she'd never given her burden to God before now. Why indeed?

She marked the moment, resolving in her heart and mind that she was ready for a different kind of life. One that sought the approval of God and not man. One that was flooded with hope.

Lord, I want to please You in all I do. For in
that kind of life, there is real hope. Amen. —AH

Help My Unbelief!

But despite all the miraculous signs Jesus had done,
most of the people still did not believe in him.
JOHN 12:37 NLT

Sometimes people are guilty of thinking, *Boy, I wish God would do some big miracles—ones that would show people His might and power and who He really is!* Maybe the person calling out for more signs and wonders is you. We've all been there. Why? Because doubting comes all too easily to humans, even Christians.

But we can see from scripture that God did miracles throughout the Old Testament. And when Jesus came, He gave us many miraculous signs. And yet many people still did not believe in Him. They did not embrace His truth and grace and hope.

If we will prayerfully look around us—really look with spiritual eyes—we will see that God does miracles all the time. We simply refuse to acknowledge them for various reasons. There will always be a reason to blow off a supernatural event. Always.

Maybe a good life prayer could arise from the latter part of this scripture passage: "Jesus said to him, 'If you are able!—All things can be done for the one who believes.' Immediately the father of the child cried out, 'I believe; help my unbelief!' " (Mark 9:23–24 NRSV).

Lord, sometimes I am guilty of writing off a miracle as a mere coincidence. Please give me discernment in every part of my life, and help me to acknowledge all Your divine wonders! Amen. —AH

Forgive Me!

He was despised and rejected and forsaken by men, a Man
of sorrows and pains, and acquainted with grief and sickness;
and like One from Whom men hide their faces He was despised,
and we did not appreciate His worth or have any esteem for Him.
ISAIAH 53:3 AMPC

Penelope had a green thumb, and people often said she had the most beautiful garden in the whole neighborhood. It contained lush flowers, trees, and shrubs to swoon over along with fountains and quaint walkways. And it was dotted with plenty of benches so people could take a seat in the verdant splendor.

Then one day, when Penelope was out for the afternoon, a neighbor came over and bulldozed her whole garden. To the ground. Leaving nothing but a pile of rubble. The police as well as the news crews who showed up to cover the bizarre story asked the neighbor why he did such a cruel thing. The man had no answer except to pridefully raise his nose and say, "I despise gardens."

Maybe this story reminds us a little of what humans did to the Savior. Jesus showed up with all things beautiful—truth and mercy, grace and hope, love and eternal life. And what did we do with all that glory? We rejected and despised it all. We raised our noses and then sought to destroy what had brought mankind the greatest hope ever known.

Lord, forgive me for the times I have walked
away from Your exquisite love. Amen. —AH

May We All Choose Wisely

Their talk is foul and filthy like the stench from an open grave. Their tongues are loaded with lies. Everything they say has in it the sting and poison of deadly snakes.

ROMANS 3:13 TLB

Words can do so many things. They can gather or separate. They can educate and uplift. They can sting like a viper and ruin a reputation in a moment. They can end a friendship in seconds, or they can heal an estranged relationship. They can welcome or snub. They can encourage a person who is living in loneliness and despair and bring them genuine hope. They can build a person up or break them into pieces. Words can be wise and full of truth, or they can be riddled with lies and flattery, pride and manipulation. They can bring love or hate, peace or war. They can challenge, praise, inspire, and delight like an unexpected fragrant breeze, or they can be as foul as the smell from an open grave. Yeah, that too.

God gives us a choice with our words every single day, and each word makes a difference. May we all choose wisely. . . .

Father God, let my words be wise, full of truth and compassion and love. Let my words always be pleasing to You. In Jesus' holy name I pray. Amen. —AH

Snapshots

*I have fought the good fight, I have finished the race,
I have kept the faith. From now on there is reserved for
me the crown of righteousness, which the Lord, the righteous
judge, will give me on that day, and not only to me but
also to all who have longed for his appearing.*

2 TIMOTHY 4:7–8 NRSV

Going through old photo albums can be loads of fun. You might find snapshots from a much-loved vacation or a treasured moment with grandparents or a time when your entire family was gathered around the Christmas tree. But then there are the photos where someone caught you coming out of the bathroom without a stitch of makeup on and wearing the shabbiest robe you own! Not so good. Or you might come across photos of someone who is no longer a part of your life—perhaps because of a move, a divorce, or a death. Those are the hardest ones to look at. Photos can chronicle our whole lives—from birth to death.

What will our soul-snapshots look like from beginning to end? Will they show a life of love and redemption and hope? Or something else? What would the Lord like that album to be full of?

Something to ponder. Something to pray about. Maybe even right now. . .

---

*Lord, I want my life to reflect You. I want to keep the
faith and finish the race well, so You can greet me
in heaven with, "Well done!" Amen. —AH*

34

All Those Bass Notes

Love will never invoke fear. Perfect love expels fear,
particularly the fear of punishment. The one who fears
punishment has not been completed through love.

1 JOHN 4:18 VOICE

When we're watching a scary part of a movie and the film plays some bass notes, going lower and lower and lower, well, we start to scoot to the edge of our seats. We get worried something bad is about to happen. In real life, we might hear a lot of bass notes. But waking up in the morning and going to bed at night riddled with fear is not a good way to live. Perfect love for God will drive out every kind of fear. Knowing the Lord is our advocate and not our enemy is a great place to start. He is not hoping to pounce on us for every error, but instead He chooses to love us back into a place of peace and joy.

May we ever rest in the strength and justice and power and love of our good God.

I can't keep running on the fumes of fear, Lord.
Give me perfect love for You. That way, I can wake
up not with dread but with anticipation. I love You,
Lord, and I put my trust in You! Amen. —AH

Anything but Grand!

For such men are false apostles, deceitful workmen,
disguising themselves as apostles of Christ. And no wonder,
for even Satan disguises himself as an angel of light. So it is
no surprise if his servants, also, disguise themselves as servants
of righteousness. Their end will correspond to their deeds.
2 CORINTHIANS 11:13–15 ESV

Franny walked up the stairs in her house for what felt like the billionth time, but this time she noticed something odd she'd never seen before. She squatted down and gave the step a close-up look. Because of the light play on the stairs, Franny had never noticed that an area just below one of the steps was painted a different color. How could that be? She showed her husband, and he marveled too that they had never seen the mistake. The oddity turned into a family joke—the grand illusion that they had all missed for years!

According to scripture, spiritual illusions are at play in our world too. Some—as 2 Corinthians reminds us—come from false prophets and some come from the enemy of our souls, Satan. He can masquerade as an angel of light, fooling the masses. He can even fool lifelong Christians. May we never succumb to this grand illusion that is anything but grand!

Dearest Lord, please keep me safe
from any kind of darkness that is
masquerading as light! Amen. —AH

Give It Up

*For all have sinned and fall short of the glory of God,
and are justified by his grace as a gift, through
the redemption that is in Christ Jesus.*
ROMANS 3:23–24 ESV

One could say that the woman had a hate-hate relationship with dust. Just as soon as she'd clean her house spick-and-span, it became all dusty again. Even after an extra-deep spring cleaning, she saw the sunlight streaming through the windows showing off trillions of particles floating in the air like impish dust fairies. Oy! So she threw up her hands in utter resignation and spent the rest of the day binge-watching her favorite TV show.

And that is the way it feels when we try and try to clean up our spiritual lives. Or maybe we try to convince ourselves that we are good enough all on our own without the Lord's redemptive and supernatural cleanup. But finally—if we look at our lives through the pure streaming light of Christ—we will see that the dust of sin is all over us, and there is nothing we can do on our own to make ourselves clean again. Nothing.

But not to fear. There's no reason to scream in frustration or wander off in a fit of despair. The message of salvation is our great hope. May we give it up—that endless pursuit to clean ourselves up and look presentable—and give in to the grace of Christ!

*Lord, thank You for the hope
of salvation! Amen. —AH*

To Kiss the Face of Christ

*Then turning toward the woman he said to Simon, "Do you
see this woman? I entered your house; you gave me no
water for my feet, but she has wet my feet with her tears and
wiped them with her hair. You gave me no kiss, but from
the time I came in she has not ceased to kiss my feet."*

LUKE 7:44–45 ESV

Mothers love to smooch on their babies, so we can surmise from
our own desire to connect with our babies that Jesus' mother, Mary,
must have spent some time kissing His cheeks when He was a
baby. What a beautiful and one-of-a-kind opportunity—to kiss the
Author of life and love!

Kissing must be something the Almighty delights in too, because
as an adult, Jesus was impressed with the woman who kissed His
feet, but saddened by the man who'd invited Him into his home
without offering Him water to wash His feet or giving Him a kiss of
welcome—the custom of the day.

In heaven, we will have the opportunity to kiss the face of Christ.
But in the meantime, every cup of cool water given in His name is like
a kiss to our Savior. Every kind word and deed we bestow—all the
hope and encouragement we give, the forgiveness and reconciliation we offer, the loyalty and love we show—is like kissing the face
of Christ.

Lord, may I reflect Your divine love in all I do. Amen. —AH

Wonderful Times of Refreshment

*Now change your mind and attitude to God and turn to him
so he can cleanse away your sins and send you wonderful
times of refreshment from the presence of the Lord.*

ACTS 3:19 TLB

Once upon a time, there was a woman who got into the habit of staring at the ground as she walked along, as she did her chores, as she
spoke with others, and as she did most everything. When someone
told the woman to look up, she was amazed at what she had been
missing. Sunsets lighting up the sky in a blaze of color. Butterflies
flitting by and a great blue heron taking off. Trees swaying in the
breeze. The refreshing sight of rain in the distance amid the storm
clouds. She had missed smiles and waves from neighbors and a host
of other glories. All from keeping her gaze on the ground.

When we've truly confessed our sins, then we should take God at
His word. We are cleansed and free, and we are ready for wonderful
times of refreshment in the Lord's presence.

Yes, we should move on. After all, God has!

---

*Dear Lord Jesus, please help me not to be so bound
up in the past that I can't see the blessings in the present
and the hope You've given me for the future. Amen. —AH*

Aren't You Tired of Me Yet?

*"The Lord appeared to him from far away.
I have loved you with an everlasting love;
therefore I have continued my faithfulness to you."*

ESVEREMIAH 31:3 ESV

Have you ever been so worn out from your humanness that you rested your head on your desk and said to God, "Aren't You tired of me yet? I know I am!"

Haven't we all had those kinds of days or weeks or even years? Think of those times when the world has tried to undo your enthusiasm, your determination, your dreams, your spiritual growth in Christ, your witness, your hope. Everything. You might feel so discouraged you begin to wonder if the Lord even loves you.

Don't let the discouragement of the world or the lies of the enemy get to you. God loves us. Loves you. Even in your humanness, He loves you. Go partake of His Word—it is lit with the radiance of that love!

God knows we are works in progress on this earth. He is so kind and patient with us. Maybe sometimes we should be a bit kinder and more patient with us too. . . .

*Father God, thank You for loving me. Thank You
for Your tender patience with me. Thank You for
everything! In Jesus' name I pray. Amen.* —AH

They Scream for Love

To slander no one, to be peaceable and considerate,
and always to be gentle toward everyone.

TITUS 3:2 NIV

Have you ever known someone who seemed to talk in riddles? She could talk and talk but said very little. She couldn't share her heart. Maybe she didn't trust people with her burdens and secrets. Maybe she had learned the hard way that people could be disloyal gossipmongers!

Or maybe you've met folks who tried to shock you with outlandish things or even vulgar things, as if in some sad and unhealthy way they want to drive you away to prove they are unlovable.

A lot of hurting people out there are screaming, but not always out of anger. They wrestle with words or remain tight-lipped or try to shock others or resort to cursing because they are screaming for love—for hope.

So what do you do with humans who need help, healing, and hope but don't know how to ask for it? Ask the Holy Spirit to guide you in these difficult acquaintances and friendships. He'll show you how to offer gentleness and compassion. How to pray for them. How to love them, even if you need to do so from a distance.

Holy Spirit, I need supernatural guidance with _____.
Please show me how to be a real friend. Amen. —AH

Curbing the Crab

Let your speech at all times be gracious (pleasant and winsome), seasoned [as it were] with salt, [so that you may never be at a loss] to know how you ought to answer anyone [who puts a question to you].

COLOSSIANS 4:6 AMPC

Let's say you come home from the store and discover that the checkout person overcharged you by thirty-five dollars. You call the store up pronto and tell them about the matter. But for some reason—even though you are one of their best customers—the woman on the phone treats you as if you are mistaken. So you explain your situation again, only this time you add a bit of an edge to your voice. Then, just before the situation gets ugly, you tone things down and try to reason with her. Finally, the woman "gets" it, but not without some wrangling on both sides. After you hang up, though, you realize you could have cut the crab a bit. Hmm. If this is the case, ask the Holy Spirit how you could improve your speech, tone, or attitude the next time you encounter the same kind of situation.

Proverbs 15:1 (NRSV) reminds us, "A soft answer turns away wrath, but a harsh word stirs up anger." As Christians, we'll have a hard time heralding the hope when we don't curb the crab!

Holy Spirit, show me how to speak the truth with gentleness! Amen. —AH

Making Things Beautiful

Then throw off your old evil nature—the old you that
was a partner in your evil ways—rotten through and
through, full of lust and sham. Now your attitudes
and thoughts must all be constantly changing for the
better. Yes, you must be a new and different person,
holy and good. Clothe yourself with this new nature.
EPHESIANS 4:22–24 TLB

Emily knew her tea party was coming up in a few days, so she went into the dining room, stared at the table, and groaned at the mess. The top was covered with piles of old magazines and unwanted stuff from closets and unfinished crafts and all kinds of other, well, junk. Emily sighed, prayed for strength, and then went after it, clearing off the table. She immediately felt better getting rid of all that old stuff and scrubbing the table clean. She shook out a crisp linen tablecloth, smoothed out the wrinkles, and began the process of making what was once a mess into something beautiful and usable and full of delight.

When it comes to our spiritual lives, can we make things all pretty on our own? No. But we can allow the Lord to renew us. To cleanse us and make us beautiful and usable and full of delight.

Lord, please show me how to throw off my old nature.
I want a new attitude and a new me! Amen. —AH

43

Hope Has Arrived

[They] said to Jesus, "Teacher, this woman was caught in the act of adultery. In the Law Moses commanded us to stone such women. Now what do you say?" They were using this question as a trap, in order to have a basis for accusing him. But Jesus bent down and started to write on the ground with his finger. When they kept on questioning him, he straightened up and said to them, "Let any one of you who is without sin be the first to throw a stone at her." Again he stooped down and wrote on the ground. At this, those who heard began to go away one at a time, the older ones first, until only Jesus was left, with the woman still standing there. Jesus straightened up and asked her, "Woman, where are they? Has no one condemned you?" "No one, sir," she said. "Then neither do I condemn you," Jesus declared. "Go now and leave your life of sin."

JOHN 8:4–11 NIV

God came calling with love that day when the world wanted to condemn a woman for sin. He forgave her and told her to leave her life of sin. And the same love comes calling today. The Lord forgives you. Whoever you are. Whatever you've done. Yes, hope has arrived—His name is Jesus.

Lord God, I admit I am a sinner. Please forgive me for my transgressions, and help me to live a new life. In Jesus' holy name I pray. Amen. —AH

A Life of Hope

Stop lying to each other; tell the truth, for we are parts of each other and when we lie to each other we are hurting ourselves.

EPHESIANS 4:25 TLB

Lucia drove home with a big grin on her face. She was pretty pleased with herself since she had managed to zap her coworker with a comeback sharp enough to put her in her rightful place. Yes, the clever retort gave Lucia satisfaction. Until she got home, and the Holy Spirit gave her a holy nudge. Somehow Lucia's smugness soon melted into sorrow.

God has entrusted us with each other. He reminds us in His Word that we are parts of each other. If we hurt someone else, we hurt ourselves. When we lie or cheat or slander or do anything to harm others, we hurt ourselves. May we remember this biblical truth in all our comings and goings, that we might live a life of joy, of love, and of hope.

Father God, sometimes I am guilty of stepping into the shadows and doing what I please. When I do this, I hurt others, I hurt me, and I hurt You. I am so sorry. Please forgive me. May I so bathe in Your beautiful light that I have no desire to turn away from You. In Jesus' name I pray. Amen. —AH

A Prettier Gospel

Every word of God proves true; he is a
shield to those who take refuge in him.

PROVERBS 30:5 NRSV

A lot of people love the Bible. But when readers seriously dig into the Word of God, sometimes they come across verses that make them uncomfortable. In fact, they might get all twitchy and downright offended!

To avoid such uncomfortable and unpleasant truths, some folks choose to ignore certain passages in God's Word. Some people have actually created Bibles with portions of the truth taken out. And other groups have even decided that the Bible is no longer the authoritative Word of God, but rather a set of guidelines.

When we create a comfortable Bible and a more palatable Gospel, we sacrifice the truth. We have lost the message of hope. We cannot remake the Word of God any more than we can remake God.

Second Timothy 3:16–17 (NRSV) reminds us, "All scripture is inspired by God and is useful for teaching, for reproof, for correction, and for training in righteousness, so that everyone who belongs to God may be proficient, equipped for every good work."

May we embrace not just some of the truth, but all of the truth!

Father God, may I never follow after any group, denomination,
or trend that dilutes, changes, or deletes passages from Your
powerful and holy Word. In Jesus' name I pray. Amen. —AH

May We Walk with God

"I know your works, your love and faith and service and patient endurance, and that your latter works exceed the first. But I have this against you, that you tolerate that woman Jezebel, who calls herself a prophetess and is teaching and seducing my servants to practice sexual immorality and to eat food sacrificed to idols. I gave her time to repent, but she refuses to repent of her sexual immorality."
REVELATION 2:19–21 ESV

The world is ever whirling and ever changing. Sometimes those changes aren't so good, and lately the world seems to be remaking itself into a darker, more dangerous place. What's happening?

As in New Testament times, we are being seduced into tolerating what God calls wicked. We are calling good evil and evil good. We are fallen creatures, and we don't have the authority to dictate to God what is sinful and what is pure. If we read the Word of God, we will know what is right—what will bring us health and delight and happiness and all things good. The Bible also tells us what God says is immoral and wrong—what will bring us to ruin and death. Harsh words? They may seem that way at first, but to repent and walk with the Lord is to know a life of joy and love and beauty and hope. May we choose to walk with God.

Lord Jesus, show us how to repent, for repentance is our hope. Amen. —AH

Choose to Be Luscious!

*Blessed is the man who trusts in the Lord and has
made the Lord his hope and confidence. He is like a
tree planted along a riverbank, with its roots reaching
deep into the water—a tree not bothered by the heat
nor worried by long months of drought. Its leaves stay
green, and it goes right on producing all its luscious fruit.*

<small>JEREMIAH 17:7–8 TLB</small>

Have you ever eaten a tree-ripened piece of fruit that nearly exploded with so much luscious sweetness that you thought maybe you'd accidentally wandered into Eden?

As Christians, are we becoming like deeply rooted trees along the riverbank, producing good fruit? The kind of fruit that brings true sustenance and spiritual satisfaction? Fruit that is bursting with truth and mercy, grace and hope? Or do people see us as those greenish, picked-too-early lemons that are so sour they produce a whole-body shudder? Not good.

We do have a choice. Oh, may we choose to be luscious!

*Dear God, I want my witness to be irresistible when I go
out into the world. I want to be full of Your goodness and
compassion, truth and hope. Please show me how to produce
good fruit. I am listening. In Jesus' name I pray. Amen.* —AH

Christ Is Not Diminished

For if, after they have escaped the defilements of the
world through the knowledge of our Lord and Savior Jesus
Christ, they are again entangled in them and overcome,
the last state has become worse for them than the first. For
it would have been better for them never to have known the
way of righteousness than after knowing it to turn back from the
holy commandment delivered to them. What the true proverb
says has happened to them: "The dog returns to its own vomit,
and the sow, after washing herself, returns to wallow in the mire."
2 PETER 2:20–22 ESV

Lately, even strong Christ-followers seem to be either falling from grace or simply walking away from Christianity. At first we might be shocked, then discouraged, and perhaps later even influenced by their behaviors. But if ministers, singers, authors, sports personalities, or even trusted mentors fall from grace or suddenly denounce their faith, Christ is still on the throne. His supernatural power, His divinity, His authority, and His sacrificial work on the cross are not diminished. Every last one of us is fallible, and so we should not be putting our faith and hope in anyone but the One who has never sinned and the One who will never fail—Jesus Christ.

Lord, may I never be influenced by the people who walk away
from You, but instead pray for them that they might come back
into Your arms of mercy, hope, and grace! Amen. —AH

Discombobulated

*Don't fret or worry. Instead of worrying, pray. Let petitions
and praises shape your worries into prayers, letting God
know your concerns. Before you know it, a sense of God's
wholeness, everything coming together for good, will come
and settle you down. It's wonderful what happens when
Christ displaces worry at the center of your life.*

Philippians 4:6–7 msg

When Elena texted, her efforts usually went all haywire. She upset other people, not meaning to, and then she upset herself trying to apologize. She tried making friends on social media, but the brutal candor sometimes gave her a meltdown. Elena would call people on the phone and then get discombobulated, assuming they were in a hurry and didn't have time for her. Then she decided just to have lunch with a friend. It went pretty well, but by the time she'd driven home, she'd picked apart every simple thing in the conversation until she concluded that her friend hated her!

Elena dropped on the couch and truly gave everything to God. Her ineptitude in friendships. Her bone-tiredness over life in general. She talked with her Lord for so long she lost track of time, and He settled her down, giving her a generous helping of wonderful. Before she knew it, a sense of God's wholeness moved over her, and she knew everything would be taken care of. Life. Friendships. Everything. . .

*Thanks, God, for caring, even about
my relationships. Amen. —AH*

Our Hearts Sigh

Come with me from Lebanon, my bride. Leave Lebanon behind, and come. Leave your high mountain hideaway. Abandon your wilderness seclusion, where you keep company with lions and panthers guard your safety. You've captured my heart, dear friend. You looked at me, and I fell in love. One look my way and I was hopelessly in love! How beautiful your love, dear, dear friend—far more pleasing than a fine, rare wine, your fragrance more exotic than select spices. The kisses of your lips are honey, my love, every syllable you speak a delicacy to savor. Your clothes smell like the wild outdoors, the fresh scent of high mountains. Dear lover and friend, you're a secret garden, a private and pure fountain. Body and soul, you are paradise, a whole orchard of succulent fruits—ripe apricots and peaches, oranges and pears; nut trees and cinnamon, and all scented woods; mint and lavender, and all herbs aromatic; a garden fountain, sparkling and splashing, fed by spring waters from the Lebanon mountains.
SONG OF SOLOMON 4:10–15 MSG

God has blessed humanity with so much goodness—the magnificent beauty of creation, a variety of delectable foods, the supernatural ability to create alongside the Almighty, the hope-filled offering of redemption through Christ, and the sacred romantic love between a man and a woman. Our hearts should sigh and our souls rejoice. May we give thanks daily for these glorious gifts!

Thank You, God, for the many gifts You've provided, including romantic love! Amen. —AH

We Understand but a Little

There are three things that amaze me—no, four things
that I don't understand: how an eagle glides through
the sky, how a snake slithers on a rock, how a ship
navigates the ocean, how a man loves a woman.
Proverbs 30:18–19 nlt

A haughtiness slithers its way into the mind of man when it comes to science and knowledge. We tend to think pretty highly of ourselves. Yes, we can put a man on the moon, but can we make a moon or the stars? We manage to erect monstrous buildings, but we are merely using resources that have been gifted to us by God. We fly hither and yon, but do we really fully comprehend the "how" of it? Truly, the more we discover, the more we come face-to-face with our ignorance. Perhaps a mark of true intelligence is admitting one's deficiencies in knowledge, understanding, and wisdom.

In other words, we understand so little of life, really, and yet God sweeps in with power and majesty. Instead of almost deifying man's accomplishments, we should be sighing in awe, praising and thanking and rejoicing over the Source of all creation.

Lord, forgive us for our arrogant thoughts and
prideful ways. I am in awe of You and Your majesty.
You are worthy to be praised! Amen. —AH

Lay It Down!

*Let him have all your worries and cares,
for he is always thinking about you and
watching everything that concerns you.*

1 PETER 5:7 TLB

Zoe had taken yet one more insult from her new boss, and she was a minute away from blowing her stack. If she didn't love Jesus, she would give the woman a verbal thrashing. But she did love Jesus, and she knew He would want her to find another way to solve the problem. So Zoe thought, *On my drive home, I will lay it down and give it to the Lord.*

Then when she got home, she found the dishes piled high, even though her teenaged kids had promised to help with the cleanup. Her husband phoned to say he would be home late—again—and her feet were on fire with bunion pain!

The words kept coming back to her, over and over: *"Lay it down, Zoe. Lay it down. Lay those burdens down at the feet of Jesus."* Then she memorized a scripture she knew she could use daily. "Let him have all your worries and cares, for he is always thinking about you and watching everything that concerns you."

And Zoe did lay it all down. What do you have to lay down before Jesus?

*Lord, I get so frazzled and tired. I need to tell
You all my troubles. I know with You, now is
always a good time to talk. Amen. —AH*

Paradise Regained

The woman said to the serpent, "We may eat fruit from the trees in the garden, but God did say, 'You must not eat fruit from the tree that is in the middle of the garden, and you must not touch it, or you will die.' " "You will not certainly die," the serpent said to the woman. "For God knows that when you eat from it your eyes will be opened, and you will be like God, knowing good and evil."

GENESIS 3:2–5 NIV

Was it June's imagination, or did the whole world seem to be spinning out of control? People were saying anything they pleased to each other, no longer caring how their words might wound. To June, evil seemed to flourish in ways that decades ago would have been unheard of. Justice seemed to be flailing, joy in question, and peace a distant memory.

Well, June is absolutely right. The world is indeed spinning out of control. It started the day the first couple decided that God wasn't enough. That He wasn't God enough for them. That's when paradise was lost. It sounds so sad—what hope is left for any of us then?

Humankind does have hope—more than we could imagine and more than we deserve. We have a Savior named Jesus Christ, and He has come for all mankind. To save us, to help us, and to take us home to heaven. Hope can't be any more beautiful than that.

Thank You, Jesus, for being my Savior and Lord! Amen. —AH

Changing the Mind of God

In those days Hezekiah became sick and was at the point of death. And Isaiah the prophet the son of Amoz came to him, and said to him, "Thus says the LORD: Set your house in order, for you shall die, you shall not recover." Then Hezekiah turned his face to the wall and prayed to the LORD, and said, "Please, O LORD, remember how I have walked before you in faithfulness and with a whole heart, and have done what is good in your sight." And Hezekiah wept bitterly. Then the word of the LORD came to Isaiah: "Go and say to Hezekiah, Thus says the LORD, the God of David your father: I have heard your prayer; I have seen your tears. Behold, I will add fifteen years to your life."

ISAIAH 38:1–5 ESV

The Bible shows us numerous instances when man has changed God's mind. One of those stories is provided in this passage from Isaiah.

Can we change God? No. But sometimes we can change His mind. Otherwise, what would be the point of prayer? Do we get every answer just as we want it? No. Even Paul didn't get the answer He'd prayed for concerning his thorn in the flesh.

But the point is, we should pray to the Lord. Prayer has many benefits, and one of them is hope.

Lord, I'm so glad that You hear my prayers and always want what is best for me. Amen. —AH

A New Kind of Hope

And endurance develops strength of character,
and character strengthens our confident hope of
salvation. And this hope will not lead to disappointment.
For we know how dearly God loves us, because he has
given us the Holy Spirit to fill our hearts with his love.
ROMANS 5:4–5 NLT

The little kid placed last in the race. He knew he would never win, but he wondered, *Do I always have to be last?* His mom and dad had come to cheer him on, but he'd lost big—again. Rats!

The teenager looked in the mirror and groaned over the fresh and flaming batch of acne on her face. She was desperate to go to the prom, but she figured no guy would want to dance with a pocked-up mess of a girl like her. Phooey. She would just stay home.

The elderly man sat on the old porch swing, waiting for his grown kids to stop by for a visit, but they never came, even when they promised. He tried to be upbeat about it, but sometimes he broke down in tears.

So often this world brings every kind of disappointment. Some we can see coming, and others take our breath away.

Romans reminds us of the hope of salvation. There is no other hope on earth like it, and it does not bring disappointment.

Dearest Lord Jesus, I am so thankful
for the hope of salvation. Amen. —AH

Haughtiness

*He also told this parable to some who trusted in themselves
that they were righteous, and treated others with contempt:
"Two men went up into the temple to pray, one a Pharisee and
tlhe other a tax collector. The Pharisee, standing by himself,
prayed thus: 'God, I thank you that I am not like other men,
extortioners, unjust, adulterers, or even like this tax collector.
I fast twice a week; I give tithes of all that I get.' But the tax
collector, standing far off, would not even lift up his eyes to heaven,
but beat his breast, saying, 'God, be merciful to me, a sinner!'
I tell you, this man went down to his house justified, rather than
the other. For everyone who exalts himself will be humbled,
but the one who humbles himself will be exalted."*

Luke 18:9–14 ESV

Once you've encountered a prideful person, you find yourself making evasive maneuvers so you don't have to deal with them. Prideful people tend to know it all. In fact, sometimes you can't get a word in edgewise! And by the time you disengage from their company, you feel tired or insulted or angry.

So you make a run for it. Hmm. Makes you wonder how many times people have run from us for the same reason!

Yes, humility is what God wants from us. That quality is what will make us peaceful people and powerful witnesses. Humility will help shine the light of hope.

Lord, teach me to be humbler! Amen. —AH

In God We Trust

*Now the Spirit expressly says that in later times some
will depart from the faith by devoting themselves
to deceitful spirits and teachings of demons.*
1 TIMOTHY 4:1 ESV

Tears streamed down Hallie's cheek. She was so disappointed she couldn't seem to have a bigger impact when it came to witnessing for Christ. She had faithfully shared the Gospel message, but sometimes discouragement came for a visit and didn't want to leave. One of her friends had just decided to leave the faith and become an atheist. Some of her coworkers openly laughed at her for going to church. And even some of her relatives were now romancing a plethora of philosophies, practices, and life choices that were anything but godly.

Even though the Gospel message is wonderful and hope-filled, in the end, we can't save anybody. That is God's job. We can show people the hope we have in Christ. We can pray for them to be moved by the power of the Holy Spirit. We can live a life that reflects Christ. But others must make a choice. In the meantime, we can do what is still printed on our American currency: "In God we trust!"

*Thank You, Lord, that You love people even
more than I do and that I can put my trust
in You—for everything! Amen. —AH*

Dad's Little Treasure

Let them make Me a sanctuary,
that I may dwell among them.
EXODUS 25:8 AMPC

The widower father listened closely to his little girl as she talked about dolls and tea parties. He sat in one of the tiny chairs—which he had built for her—and contentedly sipped some watery tea with his little gal. He mended the teacups when they got broken. In fact, truth be known, he would do just about anything for her, because he loved her so dearly.

Sometimes when he and his daughter played together with such happiness, he had to turn away his face, because he got a little embarrassed about the mist in his eyes. Sometimes his daughter would move her chair closer to his, an action that never failed to make him smile.

Obviously, the father in this story is over the moon for his little girl. She is his treasure. Our hearts long to know that this is the story of us and God. Could He really feel this way about us—you and me? Yes, even more. Much more. God has always wanted to dwell among us. He loves us dearly. In fact, He is over the moon. . . .

I get teary-eyed, Lord, when I think of how
much You love me. I love You with
all my heart. Amen. —AH

The Divine Giver

*Let the peace of Christ keep you in tune with each other, in step
with each other. None of this going off and doing your own thing.
And cultivate thankfulness. Let the Word of Christ—the Message—
have the run of the house. Give it plenty of room in your lives.
Instruct and direct one another using good common sense. And
sing, sing your hearts out to God! Let every detail in your lives—
words, actions, whatever—be done in the name of the Master,
Jesus, thanking God the Father every step of the way.*

Colossians 3:17 msg

Some women turn out to be teachers, doctors, moms, explorers, accountants, scientists, gymnasts, and builders to name a few. They are born with gifts, and they want to use them all. But for what purpose? Use the gifts for whom? Good questions to ask. Hopefully our answer leads to the Lord, since He is the Giver of those many talents.

Yes, whatever God gives us to do, may we do it with all our hearts. May we hike, decorate, wash, build, raise our children, design, clean, landscape, knit, babysit, rock-climb, compose, race, pilot, plant, and sing—all to the glory of God. And may we thank the Lord every step of the way. Thanksgiving is where hope and joy reside!

*Thank You, Lord, for giving me talents. May we
delight in those gifts together! Amen. —AH*

A Harvest of Hope

*You visit the earth and saturate it with water; You greatly enrich
it; the river of God is full of water; You provide them with grain
when You have so prepared the earth. You water the field's furrows
abundantly, You settle the ridges of it; You make the soil soft
with showers, blessing the sprouting of its vegetation. You crown
the year with Your bounty and goodness. . . . The meadows are
clothed with flocks, the valleys also are covered with grain;
they shout for joy and sing together.*
PSALM 65:9–11, 13 AMPC

Delights abound at harvesttime and in all the months surrounding
this bountiful season. There are the softening and nourishing ef-
fects of spring rain showers. The pastures that drip with dew, lit like
jewels by the morning sun. The fields of ripening grain that dip and
sway in the gentle breeze, the meadows dotted with meandering
herds of sheep and cattle. Growing times and harvesttimes are filled
with such good things and such a golden hope. May the world find
us rejoicing in every season under the sun!

*My dearest Lord, I praise You for Your harvest of hope,
not only in the fields and meadows but in the bountiful
way You bring hope to our hearts. Amen. —AH*

Invite Hope In

*May the God of hope fill you with all joy and
peace in believing, so that by the power of
the Holy Spirit you may abound in hope.*

ROMANS 15:13 ESV

Dear Hope: I am sending you an invitation. You are cordially invited to enter my situation. It's not pretty right now. In fact, it's somewhat ugly. But I believe, if you'll show up, things will turn around in a hurry, so I invite you to be my guest of honor.

I would encourage you to bring your friend Joy with you when you come. The two of you together will lift the spirits of all in attendance. No doubt you'll give me the courage to speak to mountains and to see them move, in Jesus' name. You'll give me faith to believe for the impossible, even the really big things like healing for cancer or the restoration of a broken marriage.

Hope, I'm proud of you! You've been around for thousands of years, changing lives. You've made it through wars, famines, earthquakes, hurricanes, and spiritual persecution. There's no telling how many millions of people you've impacted or how many lives you've changed. I know you come straight from the Lord (and He was good to think of you!), so I can trust you when you say better days are coming.

Thanks for always showing up when I need you!

*Lord, I'm so grateful I can invite hope into my situation,
no matter how bleak it looks. I'll keep my eye on the prize
and hope in my heart. Thank You, Father! Amen. —JT*

He'll Do What He Says

*He was fully convinced that God is
able to do whatever he promises.*
ROMANS 4:21 NLT

Whatever. Isn't that a fascinating word? When the Bible says that God is able to do "whatever" He promises, it's clear the "whatever" includes many, many promises—things both seen and unseen.

You can trust God with your whatevers. He's got a handle on them. And because He's got a handle on them, you can rest assured He'll do what He's promised. That should bring you great hope, woman of God! The Creator of the universe cares deeply for you, His child.

Angela wasn't so sure. She had a lot of "whatevers" in her world. For years she asked God to help her mend a broken friendship. And take care of her financial woes. And bring Mr. Right into her life. These things took a lot longer than she anticipated, but—even in the hard times—Angela refused to give up. The things she hoped for arrived, not in her timing, but in God's. Through it all, she learned that His hopes and dreams for her were even greater than the ones she'd had for herself.

---

*I know You have big things planned for me,
Father. I won't get ahead of You. I'll trust
Your plan and Your timing. Amen.* —JT

His Unfailing Love

The eyes of the LORD are on those who fear him,
on those whose hope is in his unfailing love.
PSALM 33:18 NIV

Martha took a seat in the rocker and leaned back until she felt comfortable, her gaze on the parking lot of the retirement home. The early morning chill caused a shiver. She pulled her sweater closer.

In that moment, as the crisp morning air settled over her, a somber feeling wrapped itself around her. Martha thought about her son and daughter-in-law, who lived hundreds of miles away. She could barely remember the last time they'd come for a visit. And her sister, Twila? Though she lived only a few miles away, a falling-out had caused her to stop visiting altogether. Hopelessness settled over Martha.

Moments later, a friend joined her on the porch. "Deep in thought, Martha?" Nettie asked.

"Mm-hmm." Martha's thoughts shifted to the beautiful friendships she experienced every day at the retirement center. How many precious, wonderful friends she'd come to know since moving in. Instead of allowing hopelessness to overtake her, Martha whispered up a prayer of thanks.

No doubt you've experienced loneliness. It can lead to hopelessness if allowed to fester. Today, take time to thank the Lord for His unfailing love and the many ways He has filled the emptiness in your life.

I'm grateful for the friends, loved ones,
and pets You've sent my way, Lord. Amen. —JT

Him, Not Me

I have been crucified with Christ and I no longer live, but Christ lives in me. The life I now live in the body, I live by faith in the Son of God, who loved me and gave himself for me.

GALATIANS 2:20 NIV

"It's not me. It's Him."

Say those words aloud. "It's not me. It's Him." Doesn't it bring you a great sense of relief to know that you're not in charge of your destiny? It's not your plan; it's His. It's not your efforts; it's His. It's not your strength, your hope, your claims to fame. Everything is His. You can take a deep breath, girl! Your future is in His hands. Everything good comes from the Lord, not yourself.

Controlling your own destiny might sound good on the surface. (Who doesn't want to determine their own outcomes?) But what if you got everything you ever wanted? Who would have to be pushed aside to always place yourself on top? And what lessons would you learn if you always got your own way? The building of character happens through loss and recovery.

Take a giant step back, girl! Hand the reins to God. You can trust Him with your yesterdays, your todays, and your tomorrows.

I trust You, Lord. I'll never lose hope as long as I remember that You're in charge, not me. Whew! It's such a relief to know I don't have to control my own destiny! Amen. —JT

Hopeful in Affliction

That is why we never give up. Though our bodies are dying,
our spirits are being renewed every day. For our present
troubles are small and won't last very long. Yet they produce
for us a glory that vastly outweighs them and will last forever!
So we don't look at the troubles we can see now; rather, we fix
our gaze on things that cannot be seen. For the things we see now
will soon be gone, but the things we cannot see will last forever.
2 Corinthians 4:16–18 nlt

Life is hard. You've been through struggles that would've brought a weaker woman to her knees. Be encouraged, woman of faith! Think about the many people who kept their hope alive in the middle of affliction. Think of young Stephen, who gave his life for his faith. He kept his gaze on the Lord until the end. Think of John, stranded on the isle of Patmos. In that foreign place, he wrote the book of Revelation. Consider Paul and Silas in the jail cell. Even an earthquake didn't shake their faith. They grew stronger with each test.

You're growing stronger too. It might not feel like it. In fact, your legs might feel like gelatin. But you really are becoming more emboldened as afflictions come. They are shaping you into a woman of strength, a woman of hope.

Thank You for giving me hope, even in
the middle of affliction, Lord! Amen. —JT

Steadfast in Pain

Behold, we consider those blessed who remained
steadfast. You have heard of the steadfastness of
Job, and you have seen the purpose of the Lord,
how the Lord is compassionate and merciful.
JAMES 5:11 ESV

It's easy to talk about hope when everything in your life is sunshine, lollipops, and rainbows. But when you're in a catastrophic season—when you've lost a child or a spouse or a job—hope seems unattainable. You can't even fathom trying to be hopeful.

Perhaps no one knew this as well as Job. You can read his story in the Old Testament book of Job. Everything was taken from him—his family, his home, his health, and his friends. No doubt he lost the ability to think clearly or to strategize about the future. But somehow, in the very middle of his pain, God began to restore his hope. In the end, God did a redemptive work in Job's life. His home, health, and children were restored and healing of the soul took place.

Perhaps you've walked a mile in Job's shoes. You've had a difficult life, harder than most in your crowd. And still, God has somehow managed to restore your hope. What a light you will be to many who are hurting.

The difficult seasons almost took me down, Lord,
but somehow I've remained steadfast in the pain.
Thank You for Your restorative work. Amen. —JT

The Promise of Hope

"For I know the plans I have for you, declares the LORD, plans for welfare and not for evil, to give you a future and a hope."

JEREMIAH 29:11 ESV

Brianna packed her bags and then checked her email to see if there was anything else to be taken care of before driving to the college. A note from her counselor with instructions for check-in greeted her. Brianna's heart thumped in anticipation.

"You ready, Brianna?" Her mother's voice sounded from the stairway. "We've got to get on the road."

"I'm ready." Brianna paused to survey her childhood bedroom. So much laughter had taken place here. So many fun conversations with siblings and friends. So many hopes, dreams, and what-ifs had been shared in this very spot. And now she would move to a new spot, an unfamiliar one at the same university her parents had once attended.

Brianna could hardly contain her excitement as she thought about this next leg of her journey. She had such hope for the future. God certainly had great things in store, and they started today.

Maybe you've been there. You faced a transition in your life and couldn't wait to get going. No matter where you're headed next, you can be confident in one thing: the Lord will lead and guide you all the way.

I trust Your plans for my life, Father.
How good You are to me! Amen. —JT

Faithful and Just

*But if we confess our sins to him, he is
faithful and just to forgive us our sins
and to cleanse us from all wickedness.*

1 John 1:9 NLT

No doubt you've heard the old adage "Confession is good for the soul." Confession is a good thing for many reasons, but one of the primary benefits is that it rids you of guilt. Guilt leads to despair and hopelessness, and you don't have time for that. How can you step into the future when you're so hung up on the past?

When you get something off your chest, you're free to take a deep breath without the twinge of a guilt-ridden conscience. Sharing the information with a good friend or family member also allows you to hear their take on things. Open your heart to godly advice. Perhaps you'll find answers there. And most important, don't forget to tell God. He is faithful and just to forgive the very moment you confess your sins to Him.

Confession will bring hope for a better tomorrow. When you're not bound up with guilt, you truly are free to think ahead. No more grief over yesterday. You have brighter days ahead!

---

*Lord, I have some things to get off my chest. I'll confess
them to You, Father—right here, right now. I need the
relief that only confession can bring. Amen. —JT*

69

Hope for Your Lost Loved Ones

"Yes, I am sending you to the Gentiles to open their eyes, so they may turn from darkness to light and from the power of Satan to God. Then they will receive forgiveness for their sins and be given a place among God's people, who are set apart by faith in me."
<small>ACTS 26:17–18 NLT</small>

Avery wasn't convinced her younger brother, who was in his late thirties, would ever give up drinking. It seemed every time she saw him at a family function his words were slurred and his gait unsteady. The longer this addiction went on, the harder it was for the whole family to handle. He would often call her in the middle of the night, completely inebriated.

Things came to a head one night when he lashed out over something ridiculous. Avery was ready to give up. She knew things couldn't keep going like this. Convinced she needed to put up boundaries, she stepped away. The prayers didn't stop, but she found herself more at peace as she prayed now. Her brother was truly in God's hands.

It took years, but he finally reached rock bottom and crashed hard. He ended up in the ICU with alcohol poisoning. Only then did his story begin to turn around.

Maybe you're ready to give up hope for a loved one in bondage. Space is good, but don't stop believing. Don't stop hoping. This situation isn't too big for God.

I'm so glad I don't have to be the fixer, God! Amen. —JT

Strength in Hope

But they who wait for the Lord shall renew their strength;
they shall mount up with wings like eagles; they shall
run and not be weary; they shall walk and not faint.
Isaiah 40:31 esv

Have you ever thought about where an eagle's strength comes from? It comes from soaring over its circumstances. If he didn't mount up and take to flight, his strength would wane, his wings would grow frail.

The same happens to you. When you lose your hope, when you sit around on the sofa scrolling through social media and ignoring life's real issues, your strength is zapped. You forget how to maintain the kind of strength necessary to conquer foes and zap mountains.

God doesn't want to see you wilting like a flower on the vine. He wants you strong like an eagle. Sure, it means you'll have to keep running when you don't feel like it. It means you can't give up, even when you're wiped out. And yes, you'll have to spread those wings and fly when you'd rather drag your feet through the mud. But with every mile you clock, you'll grow stronger and stronger and your hope will burst forth like a bud breaking through the soil in springtime.

I won't wilt, Lord! I'll stay strong so that
I can soar on eagles' wings. Amen. —JT

Where I'm Meant to Be

Now may the God of peace, who through the blood of the eternal covenant brought back from the dead our Lord Jesus, that great Shepherd of the sheep, equip you with everything good for doing his will, and may he work in us what is pleasing to him, through Jesus Christ, to whom be glory for ever and ever. Amen.
HEBREWS 13:20–21 NIV

From the time she was a little girl, Dawn knew exactly what she wanted to be when she grew up: a nurse. She could envision herself at the bedside of sick patients, caring for their every need. Unfortunately, life took Dawn in a completely different direction. As a foster mom she took her nurturing skills to a new level. One of the children was on a feeding tube. Another child had a learning disability.

It didn't take long for Dawn to see that God was using her, albeit in a different setting than she originally envisioned. Instead of grieving over the opportunities she'd missed, Dawn began to thank God for using her in a fresh, unexpected way.

Maybe you can relate to Dawn's story. Your hopes and dreams for your career didn't come true. Take a look at how God has used you. What lovely surprises He has sent your way. Aren't you grateful for them?

Lord, thank You for working through me in fresh, exciting ways. I give myself to Your service, Father. Amen. —JT

Surrounded

Many are the woes of the wicked, but the LORD's
unfailing love surrounds the one who trusts in him.
PSALM 32:10 NIV

No doubt the Israelites felt a sense of hopelessness as they faced the Red Sea. With the Egyptians bearing down on them from behind and the waters filling the sea in front of them, they had no place to turn. . .but to God. In His infinite mercy, the Lord parted the waters of the Red Sea. Can you imagine the collective gasp as the Israelites—young and old—took in the wondrous sight? How they must have stared in awe.

Of course, there wasn't much time for staring. They had to get a move on. Those Egyptians weren't slowing their pace, after all.

Those precious men, women, and children made it across safely—every last one. And when their enemies thought they could do the same, God closed the waters and swallowed them whole.

He'll do the same for you. When your enemies are closing in around you and you feel there's no hope, God will rescue you. He'll restore your hope and give you a new beginning.

Look ahead, daughter of God! Those waters are parting even now.

Thank You, Lord, for giving me hope in
hopeless situations. I'm so grateful You still
part the seas for Your children. Amen. —JT

Suit Up!

*Put on all of God's armor so that you will be able
to stand firm against all strategies of the devil.*

EPHESIANS 6:11 NLT

Gina had a hard time settling into her new job at the insurance company. For one thing, the other ladies didn't seem to like her very much. At lunchtime they would head off to a local restaurant or deli, never once inviting her. To make matters worse, her new boss was extra hard on her. His patience level was low. He didn't give her time to settle in and learn the ropes. Then, to top it all off, one of her clients misunderstood a clause in her insurance policy and took it out on Gina.

It didn't take long for Gina's hope to wane. What had once seemed like a wonderful job opportunity was now looking more like a curse. Just about the time she worked up the courage to turn in her resignation, God reminded her that He had led her to this company. She managed to summon her courage and keep going. Before long, the Lord turned her situation around completely. She made friends, settled into the routine, and even got a raise.

Maybe you've been where Gina is. You've felt ostracized or overwhelmed. It's time to suit up! There's nothing like the armor of God to give a girl hope that things will get better.

---

*I'm suiting up, Lord! This is one battle
I can't face on my own. Amen. —JT*

A Time and a Season

*For everything there is a season, a time for every activity
under heaven. A time to be born and a time to die. A time to
plant and a time to harvest. A time to kill and a time to heal.
A time to tear down and a time to build up. A time to cry
and a time to laugh. A time to grieve and a time to dance.*
ECCLESIASTES 3:1–4 NLT

Life moves in seasons. In the spiritual springtimes, you're blossoming
and growing in your faith. In the summer, you're mightily used of God,
fully flowering. In the autumn, leaves tumble, opportunities dry up.
And in winter, you often wonder if God remembers you're alive at all.

If you think about it, seasons are a blessing. Why? Because they
don't last forever. If summer went on and on (if you always got picked
to lead the women's ministry or sing the big solo), you'd probably
get a big head. If winter lingered, you would feel completely unusable. Stale.

Life moves in seasons for our benefit. We need the rest that
winter brings. We need the hope of springtime. We thrive in the
warmth of summer, and learn to trust God as we let go of things in
the fall.

Whatever season you're in, don't let go of your hope. Hang on.
Another season is right around the corner!

*Lord, seasons are for my protection,
and I'm so grateful for them. Amen. —JT*

Make an Effort

Whatever you do, work heartily,
as for the Lord and not for men.
COLOSSIANS 3:23 ESV

Susan looked around her messy house and groaned. The words "It's Saturday" made their way from her thoughts to her lips. "My day off."

But judging from the condition of her home, she couldn't really afford a day off.

"Just an hour or two to rest and catch up on TV shows I've missed."

She plopped down on the sofa and settled in. Before she realized it, four hours had passed. The house was no cleaner, she was lethargic, and her want-to was completely gone.

Maybe you've been there. It's hard to get an object in motion when it's in its most sedentary state. And yes, there really are days when you simply need to rest. But if you're feeling hopeless about the condition of your home (or anything else for that matter), here are three very motivational words: Make an effort. You don't have to conquer it all in a day, but tackle one project. Then pick another one tomorrow. Before long the tasks will be done (and you'll still have plenty of time to watch those shows).

Lord, with Your help I will kick into gear today
and get some things done! I won't lose a day
to lethargy. I'll dive right in! Amen. —JT

Everyday Heroes

For God gave us a spirit not of fear
but of power and love and self-control.
2 TIMOTHY 1:7 ESV

Joanna's husband, Tristan, worked as a firefighter. Every day she prayed over him as he left for work—for protection, for courage, and for stamina. She did her best to remember that God had not given her a spirit of fear. (She didn't need to worry about her husband, but did need to remember to pray.)

Tristan never would have considered himself a hero, but the whole city saw him as one on the day he saved a man from a burning building. The story hit the news and Tristan's world changed in a day. He received awards and pats on the back, and a local street was even named in his honor.

There are everyday heroes all around you. Knowing those amazing men and women are at work every day brings such comfort and hope. Police officers, fire and rescue, paramedics, and all of the other first responders are there for our protection, our benefit. Don't forget to pray for them—for their safety and well-being.

Lord, I'm so grateful for my town's first responders. Guard them. Keep them safe. Show me how I can serve them, Father, in response to all they've done for me and the hope and comfort they've brought to my community. Amen. —JT

Work–Life Balance

And he said, "My presence will go
with you, and I will give you rest."

EXODUS 33:14 ESV

Natalia loved her job but worked so many hours that she often wondered why she paid rent on an apartment at all. She just as easily could have tumbled into one of the empty beds at the hospital and skipped the monthly rent payment.

Natalia had a hard time juggling her workload with her friendships as well. Many of those she'd once been close to had moved on to other friendships while she kept going, going, going at work. She would see others hanging out together—grabbing lunch, going to the movies on their off-days, planning birthday parties—and she would wince. What would it be like to have that kind of time on your hands? Maybe she would never know.

Maybe you can relate to Natalia. You're a workaholic. You don't know how to say no to the boss. He knows it and continues to dump more on you. Not that you really object. You occasionally attempt an objection, yet keep taking on more work to keep yourself busy.

Some people work extra hours to avoid loneliness. Others work hard to prove themselves. Just remember that hard work should never take the place of your time with God or your relationships with others. Get your priorities straight, sister!

I'll keep things in better balance,
Lord, with Your help. Amen. —JT

The Hope Line

*"Again I say to you, if two of you agree on earth
about anything they ask, it will be done for them by
my Father in heaven. For where two or three are
gathered in my name, there am I among them."*
MATTHEW 18:19–20 ESV

Back in the old days, churches had what they called prayer chains.
The chain would start with a prayer request from a person in need.
The head of the prayer chain would call the next person on the
list. Oftentimes, they would pray together over the phone. Then that
person would call the next person on the list. On and on it went,
until everyone on the prayer chain had received the news and spent
time in prayer for the one in need.

These days we have email, social media, and so on. Folks put out
prayer requests on social media or text and receive swift responses
from many. But the premise is the same: the more people you can
gather together to pray about a particular thing, the better.

Knowing people are praying generates so much hope, doesn't
it? You're not in the situation alone as long as others are joining their
prayers with yours. If you're going through a tough situation, don't
forget to ask those around you to pray. What hope prayer brings!

*Lord, I'm so grateful for the prayer warriors You've
placed in my life. Knowing folks are praying
brings such comfort and hope. Amen. —JT*

Greater Purpose

*And we know that for those who love God
all things work together for good, for those
who are called according to his purpose.*

ROMANS 8:28 ESV

Lydia wondered why she'd been put on planet Earth. On a daily basis she would question her usability and her purpose in life. "Why did God bother with me? I don't have anything to contribute. Why am I even here?"

She struggled with her identity, in part because she didn't fully understand that her identity needed to be found in Christ, not her own gifts and abilities. More often than not she could be found cutting herself down, not building her heavenly Father up.

Maybe you struggle like Lydia. You question why God created you or why He placed you in a particular job or family. You wonder if you have any worth at all. You question your reason for being.

It's time to shift your focus, girl. This isn't about what you can do (or can't do). It has always been about God's ability to work in and through you. Take a deep breath and realize that He wants to do a complete, marvelous work in your life. Will you let Him?

*Lord, I'll stop questioning my value and worth.
I'm Your child. I'm priceless and precious in Your
sight. Use me as You see fit, Father. Amen. —JT*

What's Your Kryptonite?

But he said to me, "My grace is sufficient for you,
for my power is made perfect in weakness." Therefore
I will boast all the more gladly of my weaknesses,
so that the power of Christ may rest upon me.
2 Corinthians 12:9 ESV

Superman had amazing, supernatural abilities. He could do things no ordinary man could do. But he had one near-fatal weakness: kryptonite. This mineral had the capability of depriving Superman of his powers. It was the only thing that could take him down.

What about you? What's your kryptonite? What takes you off your game or knocks you off track? Is your kryptonite bad friendships? Overeating? Pornography? Gossip? Lying? Laziness?

We all have things that threaten to bring us down, but God wants to remind you today that with Him at the helm, you have great hope. Instead of being weakened by your kryptonite, you can give it to God, who can use that very thing to make you stronger. Instead of battling it like a temptation, you can toss it into the sea and watch it sink.

There's no reason to give up hope. Kryptonite doesn't have a hold on you. You have a hold on it. . .and you're tossing it into the abyss where it belongs.

I won't let my kryptonite take me down, Father. It's nothing
compared to Your greatness. Help me get rid of it once and
for all so that hope can be restored and fear erased. Amen. —JT

What Are We Hoping For. . .Really?

*Trust in the L*ORD *with all your heart and lean not on your*
own understanding; in all your ways submit to him,
and he will make your paths straight.

PROVERBS 3:5–6 NIV

What are we hoping for? Really, truly? Is it more money, a bigger car, a nicer house? Is it a better job, a healthy body, the latest and greatest technology? We often say that God has answered our prayers when we get these things, but what if we never got them? What if our dreams didn't come true—then what?

Does our hope rely on our personal satisfaction level? Are the two intrinsically linked? Do we have to be fully satisfied to be hopeful?

What are you hoping in? What are you hoping for? Ultimately, our hope is to be like Jesus. Our hope is to be with Jesus. Our hope is built on nothing less than Jesus' blood and righteousness. We can't hope in ourselves, we can't hope in a job, and we definitely can't put hope in other people. We can only hope in our amazing Hope Giver, Jesus Christ.

I won't put my hope in the wrong things, Lord.
Whether my dreams do or don't come true, I'll continue
to put my trust in You and You alone. Amen. —JT

Hope Laid Up for You

You are looking forward to the joys of heaven, and have been ever since the Gospel first was preached to you.

COLOSSIANS 1:5 TLB

"The cancer is back."

Meg could hardly believe the words she was hearing from the doctor's lips. Surely after two rounds of chemo, this ugly word—*cancer*—was behind her. And yet, based on what Dr. Kincaid now said, she had to face this horrible obstacle all over again. In that moment fear gripped Meg's heart and she felt her knees give way. All the hope drained out of her, like beads of dew evaporating from blades of grass. She couldn't imagine going through this ordeal again. Not now, when her hope of surviving had just returned.

Maybe you've had a difficult diagnosis like Meg. Perhaps you've been through cancer or you've suffered from a terrible accident. Maybe you've been through a horrible divorce and the courts didn't treat you fairly.

Here's something to consider: Your hope in God shouldn't be based on circumstances. He has laid up hope for you in heaven, so it's available to you 24-7, day or night. Reach out and grab it, girl. Don't let anything steal your hope.

*Lord, I'll hang tight to my hope. I won't give it up,
no matter what I face. I put my trust in You. Amen. —JT*

Hope and Rest

Yes, my soul, find rest in God;
my hope comes from him.

PSALM 62:5 NIV

Kimberly was very close to her grandmother. From the time she was a little girl, she was always Nonni's favorite. (Or so it seemed to the other grandkids!) When she reached her thirties, Kimberly began to worry about her grandmother, who was diagnosed with Parkinson's. She watched the once-vibrant woman deteriorate over a period of years.

When Nonni passed away, Kimberly was wrecked. Even though she had a family of her own, she couldn't shake the sadness at losing the one person who'd always loved and favored her. How could life possibly go on without her confidante, her friend?

Maybe you can relate to Kimberly's struggle. You've placed your heart alongside another person's, and now they're gone. It's unfathomable to you that your loved one has passed on and you wonder if the sadness will ever end.

Remember, heaven is real! If you place your trust in Christ, you will one day spend eternity with those who have gone before you. They are with Jesus now and you will join them for an eternity of sheer delight in the Savior's presence.

Lord, I'm excited about heaven. I can't wait to
spend eternity with You and with those who've
already arrived ahead of me. Amen. —JT

Nature's Song of Hope

*"But ask the animals, and they will teach you, or the birds
in the sky, and they will tell you; or speak to the earth,
and it will teach you, or let the fish in the sea inform you."*
JOB 12:7–8 NIV

Monstrous ocean waves crash against a sandy shore with a steady, holy rhythm. They flow out with majesty and are drawn back with a magnetic pull that no eye can see and no ear can hear.

Thinking about the consistency of the waves should increase your hope in something—Someone—beyond what is visible to the human eye. Even though they know they will be pulled back out to sea, the waves come back for another round. They refuse to give up.

That's how the believer should live. You'll get knocked down, sure. Circumstances will threaten to do you in. But you stand firm and brace yourself for God to intervene. With an invisible lifeline He reaches down, brings you to a place of safety.

God will never allow you to be consumed by life's challenges, as long as you trust in Him. Let nature remind you that He is right there beside you, in charge of the push and pull of it all.

---

*Knowing that nature is following Your cues brings me
such hope, Lord. If You care about the ocean waves,
surely You care about me too. Amen. —JT*

Get Inspired!

Whatever you do, work at it with all your heart,
as working for the Lord, not for human masters.

COLOSSIANS 3:23 NIV

Jennifer felt passionless. As a teen she'd always been filled with life, but in her late twenties, after a couple of failed jobs and a broken marriage, she simply gave up. All of those "What do I want to be when I grow up?" questions were gone. These days, she simply didn't care. She was in survival mode, a rather hopeless place to dwell.

Maybe you've grown passionless too. It seems pointless to pursue any dreams or visions because you've faced countless disappointments and feel you'll just be setting yourself up for disappointment again—and you can't bear the thought of another letdown.

There's nothing like passionless living to squelch hope. It zaps you of your strength and your desire to overcome. It steals your energy, your sleep, and your stamina.

It's time to dream again, girl! Don't give up. There's plenty of life left in you. There are plenty of gifts inside of you, waiting to be stirred. Your days of usefulness aren't behind you. They are within arm's reach even now!

Lord, I'll confess—the defeats of my past have made me
hesitant to step out again. My inspiration has dried up.
But today I open myself back up to the possibilities,
Lord. Revive my hope, I pray. Amen. —JT

Surrounded by Optimists

*Let all bitterness and wrath and anger and clamor and
slander be put away from you, along with all malice.
Be kind to one another, tenderhearted, forgiving
one another, as God in Christ forgave you.*

Ephesians 4:31–32 esv

Who do you hang out with? Would you say your friends are glass-half-empty or glass-half-full types? Remember, the ones you spend the most time with will always rub off on you. If you draw close to optimists—those who view life through the filter of joy and positivity—you'll find your own attitude shifting in that direction as well.

Think about Mary, the mother of Jesus. She received difficult and shocking news. How she must have struggled with knowing what to say, even to her parents. Mary sought refuge with her cousin Elizabeth. Have you ever wondered why? Surely she knew that Elizabeth would give the news a positive slant. And that's exactly what she did.

So who do you hang out with? Who's encouraging you? If you're surrounded by encouragers, then repay the favor by encouraging them as well. But if you find yourself surrounded by people who chronically complain or argue, it might be time to find a new circle!

*Lord, I'm choosing to see the glass as half full. I won't be
a Debbie Downer. I'll lift the spirits of those around me,
even the sourpusses! May I have the attitude of Christ, that
I might bring hope to the people in my circle. Amen. —JT*

Train Your Brain

Finally, brothers, whatever is true, whatever is honorable,
whatever is just, whatever is pure, whatever is lovely,
whatever is commendable, if there is any excellence,
if there is anything worthy of praise, think about these things.
PHILIPPIANS 4:8 ESV

Did you realize your brain is trainable? It's true. Think of a patient recovering after a traumatic brain injury. He labors for weeks, even months or years, to retrain his brain to relearn the things he lost in the accident.

Are there specific areas of your brain you'd like to retrain? Your negative thought patterns, maybe? Your tendency to snap at people? Your addictions?

God made that brain of yours with the skill of a Master Craftsman. It comes complete with its cerebrum, brain stem, and cerebellum and serves as the master computer of the human nervous system. You are fearfully and wonderfully made. If He spent that much time focusing on your amazing computer system, surely He's up for a rewire.

Today, spend some time listing the areas of your life that need a rewire, and then ask God to do the delicate surgery necessary.

Lord, my brain drives every action—good and bad. I'll confess,
there are areas I need to change. But I can't do it without
Your help, Lord. I need a reset, a rewire. I submit myself to
that process today, Father—for Your glory! Amen. —JT

Even on the Gray Days

*Do all things without grumbling or disputing, that you
may be blameless and innocent, children of God without
blemish in the midst of a crooked and twisted generation,
among whom you shine as lights in the world.*
PHILIPPIANS 2:14–15 ESV

Kinsey just couldn't shake the feeling of gloom and doom that hung
over her like a dark cloud today. The dreary weather outside did
little to improve her mood. She couldn't put her finger on why she
felt this way—maybe a combination of things had led to her current
state of mind. But she simply didn't feel like powering through the
challenges in front of her. She'd rather hide under the blanket and
forget about life for a while, thank you very much.

It's easy to lose hope when your attitude shifts to doom 'n' gloom
mode. But you can turn things around in a hurry. With a few words
of praise and thanksgiving, you can flip the switch and change your
day. Don't let the enemy rob you of your joy. (He loves nothing more
than stealing it from you.) Keep hope alive, even on the gray days.

*No more doom 'n' gloom for me, Lord. When I feel that
cloud hovering, I'll speak to it in Jesus' name. I'll shift
my focus and watch my day change. Amen. —JT*

Are You Sure?

When I am afraid, I put my trust in you.
In God, whose word I praise, in God I trust;
I shall not be afraid. What can flesh do to me?
PSALM 56:3–4 ESV

When you put your trust in a certain outcome, you have faith that it will happen. You don't just hope it will happen—you feel absolutely sure of it.

Think about this for a moment. You flip the switch on the wall and the lights come on. You put your trust in electricity all the time. Same with your car. You put the key in the ignition, turn it, and—*vroom*—the car starts! You have this same kind of trust when you turn on the water faucet. You're pretty sure water is going to come rushing out. Turn it to the right and it's cold; turn it to the left and it's hot.

We put our trust in all sorts of things. If the weather forecaster says it's going to rain, we reach for our umbrellas. If your mom says, "It's going to be cold out today!" you reach for a jacket.

You can be even more sure of everything God has shared in His Word. You can trust that His promises are true. When someone asks, "Are you sure?" you can say without hesitation, "Absolutely!"

Lord, I'm sure of who You are and who I am
in You. I'll never have reason to doubt You,
Father. How trustworthy You are! Amen. —JT

The Power of Hope

Now faith is the assurance of things hoped for,
the conviction of things not seen.
HEBREWS 11:1 ESV

If you've ever worked out at a gym, you know the benefit of a good workout. Over time (and with much effort) your muscles become stronger. You're able to lift more weight, work out for longer periods of time, and complete tasks with less effort. Before long, you're surprising yourself with what you can do.

The same is true when it comes to your hope. The more you use it, the stronger it gets. And remember, there's power in hope. The more hopeful you are, the greater your chances of winning the battle.

Clarissa understood this truth. When facing a financial challenge, she began to exercise her faith. Things got off to a rocky start, but the more she trusted God, the easier trusting Him became. Before long, she was completely optimistic that the Lord would cover her needs.

And boy, did He! God surprised her in numerous ways. Clarissa's hope grew with every miracle. Before long, she was testifying about His goodness to all who would listen.

You'll be testifying too! Place your trust in the One who is trustworthy. He won't let you down.

Lord, I'm so grateful You are trustworthy! I place
my faith, my trust, and my hope in You. Amen. —JT

Tune Up That Car

"His master said to him, 'Well done, good and faithful servant. You have been faithful over a little; I will set you over much. Enter into the joy of your master.' "

MATTHEW 25:21 ESV

Andrea was a hard worker. Her day job kept her busy, but so did her volunteer activities with the homeowners' association and her Bible study group at church. She raced from place to place in an older model car that needed TLC to keep running. Only, she rarely took the time to give it the proper care. After a couple years of neglect, the car reached a rebellious point and shut down. At that point Andrea took it in for a major overhaul.

That's what happens when you don't take care of things in a timely fashion. Their condition continues to decline until they're no longer usable. Now think about that truth as it applies to your hope. If you get so overwhelmed with fear and doubt that you neglect to factor hope into the equation, the situation eventually breaks down. When it does, a complete overhaul is necessary. The key? Don't let things get to that point. When you sense that first little problem coming on, deal with it right then.

Lord, I get it. My hope is like a car in need of repair. I won't let it go too long, Father. I'll perform the necessary maintenance to keep hope alive! Amen. —JT

Out of the Ashes

To all who mourn in Israel, he will give a crown of beauty for ashes, a joyous blessing instead of mourning, festive praise instead of despair. In their righteousness, they will be like great oaks that the LORD has planted for his own glory.

ISAIAH 61:3 NLT

Ashes are stubborn things. Once they adhere to the skin, they're hard to remove. They have to be scrubbed away, not brushed off with the flick of a finger. Even then, they create a nasty mess on the scrub pad or cloth. They want to stick around, to leave a lasting imprint of the fire.

When you go through a fiery trial, you emerge covered in ashes, head to toe. The smell of smoke permeates your clothing, your skin, even your hair. You can't seem to shake it. But here's great news! God is going to replace your ashes with great beauty. He'll take whatever you've been through—even the most difficult circumstance—and turn it into something magnificent. Your test truly will become your testimony. And guess what? You'll come through it all without so much as the smell of smoke on you!

Lord, I've been through plenty of fiery trials. I never fail to be amazed by the way You trade in my ashes for something beautiful. I know I can trust You, Father. Amen. —JT

Puzzle Pieces

For everything there is a season,
and a time for every matter under heaven.

When Rena hit her golden years, the sands of her life began to shift. Her husband of fifty-four years passed away, leaving her alone in the house they'd always lived in together. She had almost acclimated to the situation when a fall caused her to break her hip. Surgery left her in a weakened state, and Rena agreed to be transferred to a rehab facility so she could fully recover. Before long, the whole family was gathered around, asking questions like, "Who's going to take care of Mom?"

"Take care of Mom?" she responded, her heart in her throat. "What do you mean? Mom's always been the one to take care of you!"

But she couldn't deny the inevitable—things were changing. Rapidly.

Maybe you've had to relinquish control like Rena. Things began to spiral so fast that you lost your bearings. Trust God, even in the middle of the spiraling. Don't get so hyperfocused on the changes that you miss His guiding hand. You can trust Him, even when change swirls around you.

Lord, I'm not a huge fan of change, especially when
I'm set in my ways. But I choose to put my trust and
hope in You, Father. Please help me. Amen. —JT

Find the Bread Crumbs

But now thus says the Lord, he who created you, O Jacob,
he who formed you, O Israel: "Fear not, for I have redeemed you;
I have called you by name, you are mine. When you pass through
the waters, I will be with you; and through the rivers, they shall
not overwhelm you; when you walk through fire you shall not be
burned, and the flame shall not consume you."
ISAIAH 43:1–2 ESV

Some situations are so bleak that you struggle to find a glimmer of hope in the midst of them. You look around for crumbs—anything to sweep up—but can't find anything.

Deana felt this way after a hurricane leveled her home. The monstrous storm took everything—the house she and her husband had built. Childhood photos. Precious items purchased by her grandchildren. A collection of teacups that had been passed down to her from her grandmother. Everything.

Maybe you've been through a similar storm and it has robbed you of nearly everything. You've lost your bearings. God doesn't want you to lose your hope as well. He's going to redeem this situation. Wait and see. He will take what the enemy meant for evil and use it for good in your life. Look for those crumbs of hope and hold fast to them, no matter how dark things look.

Lord, I trust You. . .even now. It's not easy,
but I choose to hang tight to You. Amen. —JT

Hope for Personal Transformation

*Therefore, if anyone is in Christ, he is a new creation.
The old has passed away; behold, the new has come.*

2 CORINTHIANS 5:17 ESV

Carolina hated the image she saw in the mirror. She felt ugly. The other women in her circle all had great figures and beautiful smiles. In comparison, she felt like a frump. Carolina couldn't deny that she was a few pounds overweight and her teeth were crooked. But she couldn't figure out a way to change that, hard as she tried. Physical transformation seemed out of reach.

Her friends had stylish clothes that looked perfect on their lovely figures. She chose her clothing based more on comfort than looks. Not that Carolina usually worried about such things. It only bothered her when she looked in the mirror or when someone made a snide comment.

Maybe you can relate to Carolina. You have the same insecurities. Remember, it's what's in your heart, not the reflection in the mirror, that matters to God. When His Word speaks of transformation, it's not a reference to undergoing a face-lift or getting your teeth straightened. He's interested in matters of the heart. Aren't you glad?

You look at my heart, and I'm so grateful, Father. I can try, try, try to be beautiful on the outside, but what good would that do if my heart was ugly? Thank You for judging me not by my looks but by my heart. Amen. —JT

Steering in the Right Direction

For you are my rock and my fortress; and for
your name's sake you lead me and guide me.
PSALM 31:3 ESV

Valerie kept a close eye on the road ahead, but the winding country lane didn't make it easy, especially this late at night. Many times she blinked and offered up a prayer that this journey would end well. A couple times she ended up on the shoulder of the road. At least, she thought it was the shoulder. The pitch-black skies made it impossible to tell for sure.

Maybe you can relate to Valerie's journey. You're behind the proverbial wheel but you can't see where you're going. You're in unfamiliar territory and scared. Because you haven't traveled this way before, it's impossible to know when the next curve is coming. So you crawl your way along the road, shivering and shaking all the way.

Doesn't it bring you great comfort to know that God keeps a watchful eye on you? He always knows right where you are. When He takes the wheel, you don't have to shiver and shake. He's got 20/20 night vision and can see far beyond that next bend in the road.

I can trust You, Lord! I'll take my hands off
the wheel and place my hope in You as You
guide me from place to place! Amen. —JT

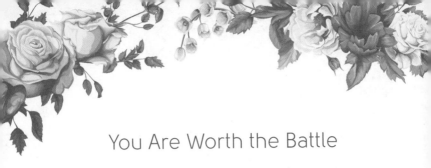

You Are Worth the Battle

For you equipped me with strength for the battle;
you made those who rise against me sink under me.
PSALM 18:39 ESV

Have you ever watched a wrestling match on TV? Those guys (and gals) really take a beating, don't they? It's hard to watch someone hit the ground over and over, taking punch after punch. You can almost feel their pain, and it's not pleasant!

It's hard to be that person who's being punched, isn't it? Maybe you've been the one down for the count with your enemy holding his fist over you. He has you convinced you can't possibly win the fight. You might as well give up now.

That's when hope kicks in. Your whole perspective changes as you look up through bleary eyes at the one trying to take you down. The words "Not today, Satan!" cross your lips and you somehow find yourself standing up once again. It takes your last bit of energy, but you're going to show him who's boss. And then—with a one-two punch—you remind him that Jesus is greater still.

Lord, may I never forget that You're greater. May I never
give up hope or stay down on the mat too long. I'll give
the enemy just what he came looking for—a real fight!
With You, I'm always going to come out on top. Amen. —JT

A Wall of Anger

Refrain from anger and turn from wrath;
do not fret—it leads only to evil.
PSALM 37:8 NIV

Anger is like a giant wall, too high to climb. The angrier you get, the higher the wall. You stare at it and wonder, *How in the world can I ever knock that thing down?* You get defeated just looking at it.

There is hope! You can knock that wall down by dealing with the foundation of it. Anger built the wall, and giving up your anger (and your need to always be right) will help bring it down again.

Who are you mad at? Why? Is your anger helping the situation or just giving you an ulcer? If you want to regain your hope, if you want to steady your breathing, you'll have to give that anger to God. Picture yourself holding it in your hands and lifting it to the Lord.

He's not mad at you for being mad. He understands. But He knows the consequences. Anger can lead to all kinds of destructive behaviors, and it's just not worth the risk.

So what's keeping you? Give up your anger and watch that wall come tumbling down.

Lord, I'm sorry I've held on to my anger for so long.
It has robbed me of my joy and my hope. Today I give
it to you. Willingly. Take it, and watch my heart begin
to heal, Father. I'm so glad to be free! Amen. —JT

Dance in the Rain

Be merciful to me, O God, be merciful to me, for in
you my soul takes refuge; in the shadow of your wings
I will take refuge, till the storms of destruction pass by.

PSALM 57:1 ESV

Stormy felt she was aptly named. In her late thirties, the poor woman went through multiple storms in a row—starting with the breakdown of her marriage, followed by the death of her father, and then a terrible accident that left her in a wheelchair for several months. Sometimes she wondered what she'd ever done to deserve such a rough season.

With God's help she persevered, but on the hard days her faith waned. Her hope seemed to slip out the window into the night.

Maybe you've been through stormy seasons too. You've faced challenge after challenge, catastrophe after catastrophe. In spite of your struggles, God wants you to dance in the rain. Instead of looking at the storms as a detriment, look at them as places to dance with your heavenly Father. There, in the shadow of His wings, you can take refuge and dance your heart out.

Lord, it seems impossible to dance in the rain. But You
can accomplish great things in my heart, even in the
middle of the storm. I offer You my hand, that I
might join in the dance, Father. Amen. —JT

Work-Related Hope

Whatever you do, work at it with all your heart,
as working for the Lord, not for human masters.
COLOSSIANS 3:23 NIV

Anita worked at an elementary school as a fourth-grade teacher. Her heart went out to the school janitor, an older widower named George. She watched him from a distance as she headed to and from her classroom with the kids. The poor man was elderly and not in the best health. Despite his work schedule and health woes, George always seemed to have a smile on his face. He would greet the kids with a grin and say, "You've got this!" whenever they were down.

Anita learned a lot from watching George. If he could keep going, so could she. His pleasant demeanor reminded her that some of the things she fretted over probably weren't important. What mattered most was the love she had for the children and the joy she radiated while with them.

How are things going at your workplace? Are you surrounded by bitter, frustrated coworkers, or have you found a friend who shares words of encouragement? No matter who you work with, God can make the experience pleasant. Ask for His heavenly intervention so you can love your coworkers the way He does.

Lord, being a light at work isn't always easy. My workplace
isn't always the sweetest environment. But I will trust You
to bring about positive changes, both in me and in
my coworkers, Father. Amen. —JT

Give from Your Lack

And this same God who takes care of me will
supply all your needs from his glorious riches,
which have been given to us in Christ Jesus.
PHILIPPIANS 4:19 NLT

She walked to the shelf and checked the jar of oil one more time. Her heart felt heavy as she realized there was only enough left to make one more loaf of bread. What would she and her son do after that? Would they starve?

A knock came at the door. The woman secretly wished a neighbor stood on the other side with sustenance, something to give her hope. Instead, she was greeted by a stranger, a man who introduced himself as Elijah. What did he have the nerve to ask for? The one thing she had so little of—food.

The widow woman did as she was asked. She gave the prophet Elijah food. In return, God filled her jar with oil and provided more than enough. She could hardly believe her eyes when provision came.

The same is possible today! When you give—even out of your lack—God restores your hope and provides all you need. So what is your area of lack? Are you willing to give, even when you're scared? The Lord blesses the efforts of the one who is generous.

I get it, Lord! I won't be stingy. You'll restore
my joy, my hope, and everything I need
if I just trust in You. Amen. —JT

Hope during Emotional Trials

*Count it all joy, my brothers, when you meet trials of various
kinds, for you know that the testing of your faith produces
steadfastness. And let steadfastness have its full effect,
that you may be perfect and complete, lacking in nothing.*

JAMES 1:2–4 ESV

Mary reached over and grabbed her sister's hands. Tears flowed
down her cheeks. She couldn't seem to control them. If only Jesus
had come in time—her brother, Lazarus, wouldn't have died. The
Savior would have healed him.

Her heart twisted when Jesus arrived four days after her brother's
death. It hurt to know He was so late. "Why didn't You come?" she
asked. "We needed You!"

Mary watched as a tear rolled down the cheek of her Savior. She
had never seen Him cry before and didn't know what to think. Jesus
stood at the edge of the tomb and cried out, "Lazarus, come forth!"
Then Mary gasped as her brother shook off his graveclothes and
stood. Was she seeing a ghost, a phantom? No, Lazarus emerged
from the tomb with the smell of death still fresh.

God is still in the resurrection business. Today He wants to res-
urrect your hope, even in the middle of the trials you're facing. Toss
off those graveclothes and emerge to new life in Him!

*I'll toss my graveclothes, Jesus!
Here I come! Amen. —JT*

Good Choices Bring Hope

Not only so, but we also glory in our sufferings, because we know that suffering produces perseverance; perseverance, character; and character, hope. And hope does not put us to shame, because God's love has been poured out into our hearts through the Holy Spirit, who has been given to us.

ROMANS 5:3–5 NIV

Good choices bring hope. That's easy to read when you're going through an easy season, when everything is going your way. But making good choices when you're in a tough season can be a little, well, tougher.

Picture this: You're down in the dumps because you've put on weight. You feel uncomfortable in your own skin. So you decide to cut back on calories or carbs until you've dropped the extra baggage. From the moment the decision is made, your hope rises. You can picture yourself being healthier and more comfortable. You have hope that you'll actually make it.

Then you mess up. You eat ice cream or chomp down a bag of chips. Your hope immediately flies out the door. One poor choice and your whole attitude shifts.

What choices are you facing today? Make the best ones you can, and even if you make mistakes, don't let the enemy rob you of your hope or joy.

Lord, sometimes I really need to make better choices. I can't blame my loss of hope on anyone but myself when I'm the one who messed up. Help me, please. Amen. —JT

Who Are You?

For you did not receive the spirit of slavery to fall back into fear, but you have received the Spirit of adoption as sons, by whom we cry, "Abba! Father!"
ROMANS 8:15 ESV

Have you ever stared at your reflection in the mirror and asked, "Who am I. . .really?" Sometimes it's easy to forget you're a child of the Most High God. You stare at the reflection and see a woman who's tired, confused, and unhappy.

Today, God wants to remind you that you are His. Think about that for a moment. As a kid, if your dad owned the whole town, would it have changed how you felt about yourself? Likely you would've squared your shoulders and told everyone, "My dad owns it all!"

You heavenly Father does own it all, from your heart to the cattle on a thousand hills. And He has adopted you as His child. You belong to the One who authored it all and owns the galaxies. When you think about it from that angle, staring at the reflection in the mirror isn't so hard, is it? Tell that woman, "Lift that chin! Be restored, hope! You're a child of the King!"

Whenever I remember who You are and who I am in You, hope is stirred in my soul, Lord. I'm a daughter of the One who owns it all! Amen. —JT

Hope after the Death
of a Loved One

*"He will wipe every tear from their eyes,
and there will be no more death or sorrow or
crying or pain. All these things are gone forever."*
REVELATION 21:4 NLT

Veronica did her best to care for her father during his final months of life. She stayed at his bedside as much as possible. As the only daughter in a family of boys, she was the designated caregiver. Not that she minded. Veronica preferred to be with her dad.

His passing nearly did her in. For weeks, she couldn't seem to keep her emotions under control. Friends couldn't seem to understand why his death hit her so hard, and she could barely give words to her thoughts to explain. Many times, she felt alone and lost. Without Dad, nothing made sense anymore.

Maybe you've lost a parent too. You understand Veronica's mindset. Whether you're six or sixty when your mom or dad passes away, the loss is just as keen. And yes, you'll feel a little lost when the head member of the family is no longer there to guide you.

God uses these situations to restructure family order, and He does so in a gentle, purposeful way. So don't give up hope. Yes, your family situation has changed, but you can find hope again even after the death of a loved one.

*Lord, I'm trusting You to see me through this season.
Restore my hope, I pray. Amen. —JT*

Hope after Unexpected Tragedy

*"I have said these things to you, that in me you may
have peace. In the world you will have tribulation.
But take heart; I have overcome the world."*

JOHN 16:33 ESV

Karen received the phone call that all parents dread: "Your daughter has been in an accident. A terrible accident. We don't know if she's going to make it."

Numb with fear, Karen and her husband drove to the large downtown hospital where they found their beautiful nineteen-year-old in the ICU, barely clinging to life. Many times over the next few weeks Karen nearly lost hope. When the doctors would say, "We've done everything we can," her heart would sink to the floor. But somehow she managed to cling to a thread of hope—and all the more as friends, family, and loved ones gathered around her and prayed. They wouldn't give up, so she wouldn't either.

Miraculously, her beautiful girl survived. She was never fully the same after the accident, but managed to return to a semblance of normalcy. In fact, Karen found a new version of joy she'd never experienced before as she retaught her daughter how to do the simplest of things.

Maybe you've walked someone through a traumatic injury. Life is different on the other side, but don't give up hope. God is still walking with you.

---

*I won't give up, even in the bleakest
situations, Lord! My faith is in You. Amen. —JT*

He Is Near to the Brokenhearted

The Lord is near to the brokenhearted
and saves the crushed in spirit.
PSALM 34:18 ESV

Brittany couldn't help herself. The tears flowed at the strangest times. It had been weeks since her husband left with another woman, but the pain was so fresh, it stung. She couldn't control when the emotions would hit, which was embarrassing.

"You deserve better," her friends said. "Good riddance."

But letting go of a seventeen-year marriage wasn't that easy, even if her husband did seem intent on making it a permanent situation.

With the help of a great counselor, Brittany finally managed to see her future as a hopeful place. Whether she remained single or God had something else in mind, she realized she could trust Him. So instead of placing her hope in her ex-husband, Brittany gave it to the One who was truly in charge, the Lord. He healed her broken heart and eventually brought her the love of an amazing godly man.

Have you walked a mile in Brittany's shoes? Don't put your hope in people. God alone is worthy of our trust.

I hope in You, Lord, not others. Even when relationships
end, I won't look to those involved to bring hope. Only
You can do that. I trust You, Father. Amen. —JT

We Are His

*For if we live, we live to the Lord, and if we die,
we die to the Lord. So then, whether we live
or whether we die, we are the Lord's.*

ROMANS 14:8 ESV

"I am Yours, Lord."

Say those words aloud and feel the thrill of knowing that you belong to the very One who created you. Aren't you thankful to know you fit? You belong! You're wanted, needed, included, and loved deeply.

When you think of the efforts God went to in order to draw you to Himself, do you get excited? It wasn't enough that you were born and lived and played a role in mankind's story. God wanted to make sure you played a role in the story of eternity as well. You're a major player, in fact.

No matter where you are in your journey with the Lord—whether you're just starting out or you've been walking with Him for years, He has a beautiful future planned out for you, one that includes streets of gold and a fine mansion. Heaven is one of the many, many perks when you're a daughter of the King.

---

*I'm Yours, Lord! Thank You for loving me enough to
draw me into the fold. I'm so excited to live out Your
plans for my life and to experience heaven one day.
It's going to be amazing, Father! Amen. —JT*

When Christ Appears

See what great love the Father has lavished on us, that we
should be called children of God! And that is what we are!
The reason the world does not know us is that it did not know
him. Dear friends, now we are children of God, and what we will
be has not yet been made known. But we know that when Christ
appears, we shall be like him, for we shall see him as he is. All
who have this hope in him purify themselves, just as he is pure.

1 John 3:1–3 niv

"A day is coming. . . ." Say those words aloud if you want your courage boosted. A day is coming when Christ will return and all things will be made known.

Do you think about that day? Does it stir your heart? You're a child of God, and when that day finally arrives, when Christ appears, you will be like Him.

On that glorious day, all of the trust you've put in Him will be fulfilled. So don't wait! Go ahead and place your hope in Him now. That way you'll be ready when that day arrives!

Lord, I want to be ready for that day. I'm Your child,
awaiting Your return. I will see You face-to-face, and all
of my troubles will fade away. I can't wait. Amen. —JT

Speak to the Struggle

"Truly, I say to you, whoever says to this mountain,
'Be taken up and thrown into the sea,' and does not
doubt in his heart, but believes that what he says
will come to pass, it will be done for him."
MARK 11:23 ESV

Crystal had a tendency to throw up her hands in defeat. She would give things her best effort up to a point; then, when the situation started looking bleak, she would fold like a stack of cards. Mountains seemed too high. Valleys seemed too low. Bumps in the road looked more like roadblocks. So she caved. As a result, she didn't make the kind of progress she'd hoped for.

Can you relate to Crystal? Do you panic when big obstacles show up in front of you? Are you scared of the mountains that rise up from out of nowhere? Are they too high to climb, too wide to go around, too deep to tunnel through?

God doesn't want you to give up, even when things get tough. If you lose hope every time you face a mountain, you'll stop making progress in your spiritual journey.

Don't stop. Speak to the mountains. Command them to be thrown into the sea—then watch as God performs a miracle. They really have to go, in Jesus' name!

Lord, I won't let the mountains intimidate me anymore. I won't lose hope when they rise up in front of me. I'll speak to them in Your name and watch them tumble to the ground. Amen. —JT

Food for Your Hungry Soul

*Your words were found, and I ate them, and your words
became to me a joy and the delight of my heart, for I
am called by your name, O LORD, God of hosts.*

JEREMIAH 15:16 ESV

Remember the old days when churches would hold picnics on the grounds? The entire congregation would gather outside after Sunday service and share in a meal filled with every good thing—casseroles, ham, baked beans, and plenty of potato salad. They would laugh, sing, tell jokes, and visit for hours on end. What fun, relaxing and enjoying one another's company.

The days of supper on the grounds might be behind us, but fellowshipping around the table shouldn't be. One of the greatest ways to feed your soul and to keep hope alive when you're in a rough season is to gather with godly friends for a meal.

Why gather around food? There, you're relaxed. You're ready to visit. Your guard is down. While you're feeding your tummy, the conversation is feeding your soul. And when your soul is fed, you regain your hope. Ah! Doesn't that feel good?

*Thank You, Lord, for the amazing godly people in my
circle. You've used them to feed my soul, Father, and I'm
so grateful for the times we spend together. Amen. —JT*

Someone to Talk To

*"But when you pray, go into your room and shut the
door and pray to your Father who is in secret. And
your Father who sees in secret will reward you."*
MATTHEW 6:6 ESV

Shh. Quiet, please! Someone is in her prayer closet and needs time alone with her heavenly Father.

Oh, wait—that someone is you! You're in your prayer closet for quiet, intimate time with the One who created you, the One who knows and loves you best. You have a few things on your mind and need to flesh them out with Someone who can give the very best guidance. You're at a crossroads and don't know where to go. You're beginning to lose hope over a situation at work. In short, you're at a loss to know what to do, so you head to your prayer closet to chat with the only One who can truly offer life-changing advice.

It's great to talk to friends. It's wonderful to pick up the phone and call a mother, a sister, a grown child. They are loaded with good advice. But when you're really in need of someone to talk to or a shoulder to lean on, go straight to the Source. He's right there, waiting to whisper hope into your ear.

*Lord, I'm here! I won't run to another. I'm coming to You
for the best possible advice. Thank You for meeting with
me and giving me all the guidance I need. Amen. —JT*

Hope Breeds Confidence

*This is how love is made complete among us
so that we will have confidence on the day
of judgment: In this world we are like Jesus.*
1 JOHN 4:17 NIV

Are confidence and hope the same thing? You can hope for something—like a kid hoping for a bike for Christmas—but still not have confidence that a bike will actually show up under the tree. Perhaps that's because we sometimes place our hope in carnal, fleeting things.

God wants your hope to breed confidence. When you place your hope in Him and not in yourself, your hands are removed from the situation and His are placed on it. When God's hands are on a thing—anything, everything—confidence is fully restored.

You can trust in Him. You can trust His Word, His promises, His love for you. When you're confident that God is actually going to do what He said He would do, a sense of expectation settles over you. Whatever happens, God will work it for your good.

Are you confident today? Are you sure the Lord will fulfill His promises in your life? If so, begin to praise Him even now, before you see the fulfillment of those promises. If you're not sure, perhaps this is the right time to ask your heavenly Father to build your hope and restore your confidence. He longs to do that very thing.

*Thank You for building my confidence, Lord!
I will trust in You, not myself. Amen. —JT*

Hard Times Will Come

But mark this: There will be terrible times in the last days.
People will be lovers of themselves, lovers of money,
boastful, proud, abusive, disobedient to their parents,
ungrateful, unholy, without love, unforgiving, slanderous,
without self-control, brutal, not lovers of the good.
2 Timothy 3:1–3 niv

Early believers faced untold persecutions. Many gave their lives for the cause of Christ, and others were tormented in unimaginable ways.

We are living in tough times too. Many believers are finding it difficult to stand up for their faith. They're losing hope—both in the cause of Christ and in society. There has never been a more critical time to take a stand for the Gospel. Even though it's hard, you must stand up and be counted. As the world spirals deeper and deeper into sin, you can rise above it. You can set an example for those who are watching. You can motivate others with the hope that is in you.

Will you take a stand, or will you crater? As you contemplate this question, think of John the apostle, banished to the isle of Patmos because of his faith. Consider Stephen, who was stoned to death because of his beliefs in Christ. If they could take a stand, then those of us who call ourselves believers in the twenty-first century can keep standing too.

I'll keep standing, Lord. I won't cave to
the pressure, even if persecution comes.
My life is fully Yours, God! Amen. —JT

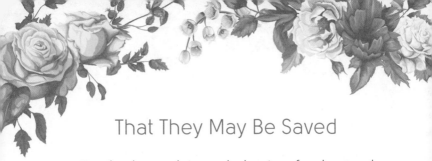

That They May Be Saved

*Dear brothers and sisters, the longing of my heart and
my prayer to God is for the people of Israel to be saved.*

Melinda loved her work as a missionary in Chile but often wondered if she was making any difference at all. Sure, the kids at the orphanage loved her and they seemed wide open to the Gospel, but many of the adults in the surrounding community were far away from the Lord.

When she spent too much time focusing on the evil going on around her—drug sales, prostitution, and more—Melinda got overwhelmed. She often wondered if the children she was working with today would one day join the ranks of those who were caught in the enemy's snare.

Maybe you've wondered the same thing as you look around you at those who are in your circle. Some are open to the Gospel, but the majority are enjoying their sinful choices way too much to take a step in God's direction.

Don't give up. Keep praying. Keep hoping. Put your trust in the Lord. Everything is handled in His timing, after all. You never know who might show up on your doorstep wanting to hear the Good News!

*I won't give up, Lord. I know You love every person in my circle,
even the ones who don't make life easy. I'll keep hope alive
that all of them might come to know You. Amen. —JT*

Born Again to a Living Hope

Praise be to the God and Father of our Lord Jesus Christ!
In his great mercy he has given us new birth into a living
hope through the resurrection of Jesus Christ from the
dead, and into an inheritance that can never perish,
spoil or fade. This inheritance is kept in heaven for you.
1 PETER 1:3–4 NIV

Valleys can run pretty deep, and Christians are not immune from trudging through them. Whether it's the loss of a child, a suicide in the family, or a devastating financial loss, a valley can be a life-altering event. And how you navigate each valley is critical.

Some believers inadvertently tumble into the deep, dark valley of addiction. Maybe you've been there. It started with a drink or two, and before long you were self-medicating every night before bed to wash away the pain of the day. Then the issue became more acute as you started drinking earlier and earlier in the day. It came to a head when the alcohol began to interfere with your ability to work and parent.

You might look at an addicted friend or family member and say, "It's impossible. They're never going to quit." Chemical addiction is a tough thing to overcome, after all. But there is hope! Every day, people quit—alcohol, drugs, pornography, and so on. Addictive behaviors are strong, but nothing is as powerful as our God. He can bring hope, even in the deepest valley.

Thank You for bringing hope in the valley, Lord! Amen. —JT

You Are Being Changed

So all of us who have had that veil removed can see and reflect the glory of the Lord. And the Lord—who is the Spirit—makes us more and more like him as we are changed into his glorious image.

2 CORINTHIANS 3:18 NLT

You are being changed. Right now. Right where you are. You're being transformed at this very instant, whether you recognize it or not.

Wow! Maybe you find that hard to believe. Every day feels like the same old same old. Changes are hard to see—in your heart or your thoughts. But from the time you give your heart to the Lord, you're being transformed into His image more and more with each passing day.

Don't believe it? Remember when you used to walk around defeated all the time? You don't anymore. And remember when you had no hope that things would get better? Now you do.

The transformation process is slow and steady, much like a butterfly emerging from its chrysalis. One day soon you'll take to flight, a beautiful butterfly. Until then, let God continue to do the work of transformation, little by little, until you are like Him in every way.

Lord, thank You for the transformation process. I want nothing more than to be like You. Change isn't easy, but becoming more like You is an honor and a privilege. Amen. —JT

Persecuted without Cause

All your commands are trustworthy; help me,
for I am being persecuted without cause.
PSALM 119:86 NIV

He never saw it coming. The missionary was on his way home from a meeting, one where multiple people had come to know the Lord. At first he didn't notice the car following him down the dirt road. The farther he drove, however, the more he began to suspect the driver of the vehicle was targeting him.

Sure enough, when he stopped at a stop sign, several men jumped out of the truck behind him and pulled him from his car. He heard the shouts, felt the sting as one of the men jerked him to the road, then felt the searing pain as his head was struck.

The rest was a blur. The doctors said it was a miracle he'd lived through the assault. Charles later learned the men were angry that he had brought the Gospel to their village. They didn't want outside influences coming in.

Perhaps you've faced persecution in your life too. Many times you've felt like giving up. It's not time to quit just yet, sister. There's still work to be done. God is your protector. He's your defender. You just stick with the program and watch as He deals with those who would seek to harm you.

Lord, thank You for protecting me when I'm persecuted,
especially when I've done nothing to provoke others.
I'll trust You to keep me safe, Father. Amen. —JT

The Rock Eternal

Trust in the LORD forever, for the LORD,
the LORD himself, is the Rock eternal.

ISAIAH 26:4 NIV

Nora and her husband, Zach, purchased a plot of land and planned to build a home. They had the plans drawn up by an architect and began the process by hiring a company to clear the land. Several trees were taken down and the soil—which was rockier than they'd guessed—was leveled.

In the very middle of the spot where they planned to put the house, a large boulder was discovered. It was poking out above the flat surface of the ground around it. The boulder needed to come out. Only one problem—it was too big to pull out, even with several men working together. They tried to split it with a wedge, but that didn't work. Finally, they resorted to using a rock hammer, which split the boulder into pieces.

The Bible says that God is the Rock Eternal. He's not going anywhere. He can't be broken, even with a jackhammer! He'll remain steady and strong, a permanent fixture in your life. Doesn't that truth bring hope to your soul?

Lord, I'm so glad You're my Rock Eternal! Thank You
for Your consistency in my life. I'm so grateful
for the hope You bring. Amen. —JT

Hope When Chaos Reigns

*For God is not a God of
confusion but of peace.*
1 CORINTHIANS 14:33 ESV

Lauren couldn't seem to get a handle on her day. It started with the news that she'd somehow forgotten to pay the water bill. As a result, she couldn't shower or brush her teeth. She scrambled to pay the bill online then rushed to work, arriving late. She walked in on an important meeting and her boss was angry. Then, just about the time the meeting ended, a call came through from the school nurse. Lauren's eight-year-old son had a high fever and sore throat. Flustered, she asked for the rest of the day off. To say her boss didn't take the news well would be an understatement.

We all have those days, don't we? When chaos reigns in your life—when all the apples are falling from the tree at the same time and hitting you on the head—where do you turn? If you're inclined to panic, hope surely seems far away. But if you pause, take a deep breath, and ask God to meet you in the very middle of your mess, He will do so. Right there in the bedlam, He can restore order in your heart and give you hope that all will end well.

*Thank You for restoring order on my crazy days, Lord!
I need the hope that only You can bring. Amen. —JT*

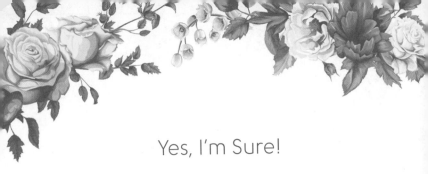

Yes, I'm Sure!

Now faith is the assurance of things hoped for,
the conviction of things not seen.
HEBREWS 11:1 ESV

Have you ever second-guessed yourself? Maybe your spouse or child asked a simple question like, "Did you turn off the stove before you left the house?" or "Did you remember to pay that bill I was supposed to remind you to pay?" and you say, "Yes, I'm sure I did." But then you find yourself tormented. Did you. . .really? Are you sure?

Doubts plague us at times, especially when we fear for our home or belongings. But we never have to doubt when someone asks us, "Are you sure?" about our faith in Jesus. We can say—with full assurance—that we are absolutely, positively, without question sure that He is who He says He is and will do what He says He will do.

"Yes, I'm sure!" is the only answer for the believer. "Yes, I'm sure He loves me! I'm sure He died for me. I'm sure my sins are forgiven. I'm sure about heaven. I'm sure of the hope He has planted in my heart."

Are you sure today?

Lord, thank You for the assurance You bring in all areas
of my life. I don't have to wonder. I don't have to doubt.
I can be absolutely, positively sure in You. Amen. —JT

If He Said It. . .

I wait for the LORD, my soul waits,
and in his word I hope.
PSALM 130:5 ESV

Do you believe in the authority of scripture? Do you believe it is the living, breathing Word of God, given for this day and age, as well as for people in days gone by?

If you believe in the authority of scripture, you have to conclude that the words you find within the pages of the Bible are as living and applicable today as they were when written. And if all of this is true, then you can take great comfort in that Word, because it offers the key to life—both spiritual and physical.

If God said it, you can count on it. If you read a biblical promise, you can take it to the bank. You can breathe a huge sigh of relief! The Bible won't let you down. Yes, you'll go through tough circumstances. They might cause you to flinch or even give up your hope for a few moments. But if you really latch on to the truth of the Word of God, you can't stay down for long. Every promise is true—and every promise is for you.

Lord, I'm so grateful for Your Word. If You said it,
Father, it still applies to my life, my circumstances,
and my dreams for the future. Thank You, Lord! Amen. —JT

Sharper Every Day

As iron sharpens iron, so a friend sharpens a friend.

PROVERBS 27:17 NLT

When Deb was only four years old, her younger sister was born. Little Maddy experienced trauma during her birth and had cerebral palsy as a result. Deb welcomed her new little sister with open arms and didn't notice or care that her sister was different from the other kids. When they got older, Maddy's disabilities became more noticeable. She struggled to walk and had issues with muscle wasting and verbal skills. Still, these things didn't bother Deb one bit. She adored her little sister and did all she could to make her life easier and more fun too.

Thinking about Deb and Maddy's relationship in relation to the "iron sharpens iron" concept from Proverbs 27:17 puts a whole new spin on things. Each made the other better, stronger, more likely to overcome life's challenges.

Who is sharpening you today? Who are you sharpening? In order to grow as a believer, you should have mentors who are pouring into you and people you're pouring into. Ask God to show you who those people might be.

Lord, thank You for the relationships that make me stronger. I want to help others grow too. I'm grateful for my mentors and for those I'm mentoring. Amen. —JT

Hope in the Face of Persecution

*And hope does not put us to shame, because God's
love has been poured into our hearts through
the Holy Spirit who has been given to us.*

<small>ROMANS 5:5 ESV</small>

The prison doors slammed behind them. Paul and Silas settled into their spot on the floor across from the other prisoners. Though jailed for different reasons than the others, these two men found themselves bound nonetheless.

"What have you two done?" one of the prisoners surely asked. "Murder? Theft?"

Maybe Paul chuckled under his breath as he said, "Proselytizing."

"Proselytizing? Never heard of it."

Before they could carry the conversation any further, Paul and Silas began to lift up songs of praise. They turned their jail cell into a meeting house. They proclaimed hope in a hopeless situation. In the middle of their praise, an earthquake shook the room. In that moment, the prisoners' chains were broken and the doors to the cell swung open.

Maybe you've used praise to break chains too! No matter what you're going through, hope arrives when you lift a song of praise, even in the very midst of the battle.

*Lord, I'm grateful for the reminder that a song
of praise will go a long way in bringing hope.
I lift my voice to You today, Father! Amen.* —JT

Access by Faith

Therefore, since we have been justified through faith,
we have peace with God through our Lord Jesus Christ.

ROMANS 5:1 NIV

Fiona kept all of her keys on one ring. When she needed a specific key, sometimes she wasn't sure which one it happened to be. She'd try key after key after key, hoping to open the locked door, only to be disappointed time and again.

That's how it is when we're working, working, working to get into heaven. We don't have the right key. It's held by Jesus, our Savior. Instead of struggling on our own, we need to learn to put our trust in Him, to accept Jesus as Lord and Savior. In that moment He will open wide the door to heaven.

Faith is the great activator. To put your faith in Christ (rather than in your own good works) means you remove your hands and say, "I can't open this door, Lord, but You can." In that moment, as you speak that simple truth, your whole life will change. Hope will flood your soul as you come to the understanding that some doors were never yours to open in the first place.

Trust Him. He has the key.

Lord, I've placed my trust in You. I need
the hope of salvation. Open wide the door,
I pray! I want to come through. Amen. —JT

The Kingdom of Heaven Is Yours!

*"Blessed are those who are persecuted because
of righteousness, for theirs is the kingdom of heaven."*
MATTHEW 5:10 NIV

When Pastor John took a team to Turkey for mission work, he never dreamed he would end up in prison. But that's exactly what happened. The rest of his team was released, but he ended up staying behind bars for several weeks until the ordeal came to an end.

No one becomes a believer hoping to be persecuted for their faith. But we live in perilous times, and not everyone is happy to hear the Gospel message preached. Regardless of the risk, Christians are called by God to take a stand. And if—or when—persecutions come, the Lord has promised in His Word that we are blessed when we are persecuted because of righteousness. And it is possible, even in the midst of the trial, to keep hope alive and to remain strong in our faith. Many Bible stories prove this point.

Hopefully you'll never face the kind of persecution Pastor John and his team faced, but trials will come. Be ready for them. Keep your head high. And keep hope alive.

---

*Lord, I'm ready, no matter what comes my way. You've made
me strong in You. I can withstand any obstacle and I won't
give up hope, even in the darkest valley. Amen. —JT*

Butterfingers

*So then, brothers and sisters, stand firm and
hold fast to the teachings we passed on to you,
whether by word of mouth or by letter.*
2 THESSALONIANS 2:15 NIV

Have you ever heard the old expression, "It just slipped right through my fingers"? When you're not holding as tightly as you should to something, the possibility of losing it at any moment is very real.

God wants you to hold fast to the things you've learned while walking with Him. Grip them tightly. Don't let them slip through your fingers. If you begin to treat His words carelessly, there will be a heavy price to pay. Before long you'll find your hope gone and your morals slipping.

Are you holding fast to what you've learned? Are there any areas of your life that could use tweaking? Maybe you're not as diligent as you once were about your time with the Lord—reading the Bible and praying. Maybe your language is slipping when you hang out with coworkers. Maybe you've crossed a line with alcohol or the kind of movies and TV shows you watch.

Hold fast. Don't let your faith slip through your fingers. The only way to keep hope alive is to hang on for dear life to what you know to be true.

*Lord, I'm holding fast. I won't let go. I don't want to
compromise, Father, so I'll cling tightly to You. Amen.* —JT

What's the Reason?

*"For you shall go out in joy and be led forth in peace;
the mountains and the hills before you shall break forth into
singing, and all the trees of the field shall clap their hands."*
ISAIAH 55:12 ESV

If someone were to ask, "What's the reason for your joy?" how would you respond? If you're a believer in Christ, if He has changed your heart and replaced your mourning with dancing, you would surely say, "It's Jesus!"

Believers should stick out like sore thumbs. The Christ-follower's jubilant countenance should be a reflection of Him, even on the darkest days. This isn't a "fake it till you make it" plan. When Jesus permeates your being, you don't have to fake it. His joy is the real deal. It's faith-building, hope-giving, stamina-producing joy that will help you make it through every situation with His power, His strength.

"What's the reason for your joy?" Why, it's Jesus, of course!

---

*Lord, You're the reason for my joy. On good days and bad,
my joy comes from You. I'm forever changed,
thanks to You. Amen. —JT*

The Sky Is Falling!

*And now, dear brothers and sisters, one final thing.
Fix your thoughts on what is true, and honorable,
and right, and pure, and lovely, and admirable. Think
about things that are excellent and worthy of praise.*

Philippians 4:8 nlt

Have you read the story of Chicken Little? She went around crying, "The sky is falling! The sky is falling!"

Maybe you've felt like Chicken Little at times. With so many things crashing in around you, it really did seem like your proverbial sky was falling. When you're facing obstacles of any kind, your perspective can change absolutely everything. You can respond (as Chicken Little did) by screaming, "All is lost!" or you can place your trust in God Almighty and hear Him whisper, "I've got this."

When the Lord takes hold of the skies, they can't possibly fall. The enemy will work overtime to make it look as if they're coming down any moment, but God has a steady hand on them and they won't touch you. So what's it going to be, daughter of God? Chicken Little or woman of faith? Put your trust in the One who holds the skies (and the whole world) in His hands.

---

*Lord, I don't want to be a Chicken Little.
My skies aren't really falling. You have a tight
grip on them and I know I can trust You. Amen. —JT*

Hang On!

Let us hold unswervingly to the hope we profess,
for he who promised is faithful.
HEBREWS 10:23 NIV

If you've seen the movie *Titanic*, you know there's a scene at the end where Jack—the story's hero—is holding on to the edge of a wood plank, trying to survive in the icy cold waters. The story's heroine implores him to hang on. She is sure they will both make it as long as she encourages him.

Tragically, the icy waters take Jack's life. He slips into the Atlantic, never to be seen again. Yet there is something inspiring about Rose's resolve to encourage him despite the grim circumstances.

If your life depended on it, could you hang on like that? It's hard to know unless you're in that type of situation, isn't it? God wants you to hold on to your hope just as you would cling to that life raft. Don't let go. There will be days you're so overcome that you'll be tempted to let it slip out of your grasp. . .but don't. Tighten your grip, even when it makes no sense. Keep holding on.

God will save you from the murky depths if you don't give up. He's the great Hope Giver, after all.

Lord, I'll hold tight, even when I feel like
letting go. Thank You for giving me hope,
especially in hopeless situations. Amen. —JT

Pressing Through

Continue steadfastly in prayer,
being watchful in it with thanksgiving.

COLOSSIANS 4:2 ESV

She pressed her way through the crowd, determination setting in. If only she could get to the Master, the one they called Jesus, all would be well. The issue of blood she had struggled with for so long could be gone in an instant. If only she could reach Him.

The crowd refused to part, so the woman found herself on her hands and knees. Whatever it took, she would get to Him. Then, just as she drew close, He turned. She reached out her hand and grabbed hold of the only thing in front of her—the hem of His garment. In that moment, healing power shot through her hand, spread up her arm, and radiated through her body. It was all she could do not to let out a scream.

"Who touched Me?" Jesus looked around until his eyes—those beautiful, mercy-filled eyes—locked on hers.

"I did, Master," she surely whispered. "And now everything has changed."

That's what happens when you reach out to take hold of everything Jesus has for you. Nothing in your life remains the same. Hearts are mended, vision restored, and hope reborn! So keep on pressing through, woman of God!

Lord, I'm so glad I reached out to touch You.
You've changed everything! Amen. —JT

Hope Begins with Jesus

They replied, "Believe in the Lord Jesus,
and you will be saved—you and your household."
ACTS 16:31 NIV

Paul and Silas—ardent followers of Jesus—were freed from a prison cell when an earthquake hit. The doors were opened and they were free to leave. Only, they didn't. They stayed behind to talk to the jailer, who was in a panic at the thought of prisoners potentially escaping.

The jailer fell trembling before Paul and Silas, petrified. His question must have seemed strange in the moment. Instead of asking, "Why are you still here? Why didn't you run when you had the chance?" he posed a completely different question: "What must I do to be saved?"

Perhaps you've heard the old expression that there are no atheists in fox holes. It certainly proved true here. The jailer listened closely as the men shared the Gospel message. Then he dressed their wounds and called for the members of his household, and all were baptized.

The story of Jesus changed everything in that jailer's life. With just one word—*Jesus*—his hope was completely restored. Not only that, but his entire family was swept into the kingdom. Talk about a true happily ever after!

God, You are so good to us! You meet us at our very
moment of panic and say, "Don't worry! I'm here!"
Thank You for never leaving me, Jesus. Amen. —JT

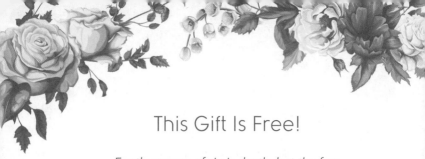

This Gift Is Free!

*For the wages of sin is death, but the free
gift of God is eternal life in Christ Jesus our Lord.*

Romans 6:23 esv

"What's the catch?" Judy asked as she reached for her wallet. "Do I need to pay some sort of fee?"

"No." The clerk shook her head. "The judge dismissed your ticket. There's no charge at all."

"No charge. . .at all?" Judy could hardly believe her luck. She'd been stopped for going six miles over the speed limit but also received a ticket for her registration sticker being out of date. It was an innocent mistake. She'd simply forgotten to take care of it the month prior. Of course, she'd gone straight to the courthouse to get the new sticker once she received the ticket. And now the judge was dropping the charges. Ticket dismissed. Judy couldn't believe it. She tucked her wallet back in her purse, thanked the clerk, and headed back to her vehicle.

Perhaps something like this has happened to you. For sure, it happened when you gave your heart to Christ. He forgave your sins, wiped the slate clean, and said, "No payment required! I've taken care of it for you." What a wonderful Savior we have. What hope He brings as He offers the gift of forgiveness so freely!

*God, I'm so grateful You've wiped my slate clean. I can breathe
easy now that You've paid the price, Lord. Amen. —JT*

Take a Chance

For you, O Lord, are my hope,
my trust, O Lᴏʀᴅ, from my youth.
Pꜱᴀʟᴍ 71:5 ᴇꜱᴠ

Esther was a young Jewish girl chosen to be the wife of the Persian king Ahasuerus. She was selected because of her beauty. Haman, the king's advisor, plotted to kill all of the Jewish people, but when Esther learned of his plan, she intervened. In the end the Jewish people were spared, all because one young woman took a chance.

Have you taken any chances lately? Have you stepped out in faith, even if your knees were knocking or your voice quivering? Sometimes the only way to get past your circumstances is to step boldly into the unknown and take a risk. It won't be easy (hence the word *risk*), but the payoff can be life-changing. You could very well change the course of history, not just for yourself, but for others as well. It will take courage, but with God on your side, you can do it, girl!

What area of your life requires intervention today? Are you willing to stand up and take a chance? Perhaps, like Esther, you were born for such a time as this.

Lord, I won't be afraid to take chances.
I'll remember that You've placed me right
here, right now, for a reason. Amen. —JT

The Tests You Have Passed

So let's not get tired of doing what is good. At just the
right time we will reap a harvest of blessing if we don't give up.
GALATIANS 6:9 NLT

Have you ever watched a marathon? The runners set off with gusto but often end up crawling over the finish line, completely worn out. Some people are so bedraggled by the end of the race that they're literally on their hands and knees. They hear the cheers and they're encouraged to keep going. (It's hard to give up when people are cheering you on!)

Take a look at all the tests you've been through. Each one was like a marathon of sorts. Spend some time examining the outcomes of the many races you've won. You have passed many, many tests with flying colors! You're a straight-A student when it comes to life's tests, in fact. Sure, you had to crawl over a few finish lines, but you made it! Kudos for not giving up!

Don't be so hard on yourself. Don't say, "I'm a loser. I can't seem to get my act together." Instead, look how far you've come. Those tests you've passed have made you a winner in God's book!

Lord, I've made it through so many challenges already.
I haven't given up. (You wouldn't let me, and neither
would the people in my inner circle.) I won't give up now.
I've come too far to be stopped. Amen. —JT

God Takes Pleasure in Your Hope

*Rejoice in hope, be patient in tribulation,
be constant in prayer.*
ROMANS 12:12 ESV

Cheryl didn't come to know the Lord until she reached her thirties. When she fell into His embrace, she fell hard. Cheryl never looked back at the woman she once was. She made it her life's mission to apply forward motion only. Because of this radical change in her thinking, her old friends and family were intrigued. Gone was the bitter, callous woman they had known. In her place was a vibrant, hopeful gal with nothing but praise on her lips. They took great pleasure in the change.

You know who else took great pleasure in it? The Lord! When He looks down at women like Cheryl, who've come through so much, His heart is filled with great joy.

Maybe you've known a few Cheryls in your life. (Maybe you are one!) Freedom in Christ is a new way of living, a new way of thinking. No wonder Cheryl couldn't help but smile. The old was in the past. The new had come. Now that's worthy of celebrating!

Lord, thank You for taking pleasure in the positive changes in my life. I'm grateful for the chance to look forward, not back, and I'm so glad my forward-thinking attitude makes Your heart happy! Amen. —JT

Out of the Rubble

Blessed be the God and Father of our Lord Jesus Christ! According-
ing to his great mercy, he has caused us to be born again to a
living hope through the resurrection of Jesus Christ from the dead.

1 PETER 1:3 ESV

Jessie stood in the spot where her house used to be. The tornado had leveled it, leaving nothing but rubble. The lump in her throat was so big she could barely swallow it down as she surveyed the property. How could God have allowed such a thing to happen? Off in the distance her husband pulled away pieces of Sheetrock and wood. "Jessie, come here!" he called out.

She made her way toward him, moving carefully so as not to get hurt. "What is it?"

He lifted a familiar photo album and brushed the dirt from the cover. Jessie could hardly believe it. How in the world had these priceless photos survived amid all this destruction?

That's how life is sometimes. Unexpected tragedy hits and we're sure all is lost. Then somehow, miraculously, God pulls something beautiful out of the rubble. Hope is restored.

What areas of your life has God redeemed from the rubble? Perhaps it's time to praise Him for the victories on the other side of the pain.

Lord, there has been plenty of rubble in my life, for sure.
But You've brought beauty from the ashes, joy from the pain.
I'm grateful for Your redeeming work, Father. Amen. —JT

God Is Doing Something New

"See, I am doing a new thing! Now it springs up;
do you not perceive it? I am making a way in the
wilderness and streams in the wasteland."

ISAIAH 43:19 NIV

So much of life depends on the flow of thirst-quenching water. Creeks, streams, and rivers draw people to congregate and build towns around them and to plant crops that grow into fields of harvest. On the other hand, to experience a dearth of water across the land can be devastating. It can make a verdant valley inhospitable. It can make what seems like a promise perilous.

Imagine that desert, dry and barren—with no hope of even a cactus flower to bloom—suddenly coming to life with bubbling pools of pure water. That is what God promises us. He is doing something new in our lives. He is making a path through what feels impassable, and He will command a stream to flow through the wilderness of our pasts, places where we had only known the wasteland of sin and a landscape of despair.

So, believe in what God can do. Have faith and bring your empty buckets to the stream. Lift the dipper to your parched lips and taste the water that is sweet and new and refreshing.

Father, thank You for Your provision, hope, and joy. Without You,
life is dry and hostile. Come into my life and quench my thirst.
You are the only one who can fulfill me. Amen. —AH

Power, Love, and Self-Control

This is why I remind you to fan into flames the spiritual gift God gave you when I laid my hands on you. For God has not given us a spirit of fear and timidity, but of power, love, and self-discipline.
2 TIMOTHY 1:6–7 NLT

When you're riddled with fear, hope takes a backseat. In fact, hope can usually be found in the trunk when fear is guiding the proverbial vehicle. Fear wraps itself around your heart and mind like tentacles. It crowds out anything and everything else.

God didn't give you a spirit of fear. Stop to think about that for a moment. If you're overwhelmed by hopelessness that's triggered by fear, you can rest assured it's not from God. The enemy is working hard to take you down, but the Lord definitely isn't the One causing your fear.

God has given you three things to counter your fear: power, love, and a sound mind. When you're operating in the power of His Spirit, when you're resting in His great love for you, when you have the mind of Christ, fear has to go in Jesus' name!

Lord, I won't give way to fear. It has no place in my life. You've given me power! You've given me love! You've given me self-control. These are precious gifts, and I won't take them for granted, Father. Amen. —JT

A Child's Trust

*Yet you brought me out of the womb; you made
me trust in you, even at my mother's breast.*
PSALM 22:9 NIV

A child trusts implicitly. He knows his mother will feed him, clothe him, and come when he cries. It never occurs to a baby to run away from home to find a better caregiver. (Can you even imagine?) He's satisfied with the one he has because she dotes on him and takes care of his every need.

What about you? Are you tempted to run away from home? Do you fall out of trust with God? Do you lose your hope and head off to other caregivers (friends, books, or philosophies)? The Lord wants you to keep your trust in Him. He's not going to let you down. Sure, you can receive wise counsel from friends, and yes, you can learn a lot from books. But ultimately, your trust needs to be rooted in the One who created you and loves you best. He's singing over you even now and making sure you have everything you need.

You were made to trust in your earthly parents and in your heavenly Father.

*Lord, I trust You. I won't run to another,
abandoning You altogether. I'll place my trust—
and all my hope—in You. Amen. —JT*

Love Brings Hope

*Above all, keep loving one another
earnestly, since love covers a multitude of sins.*
1 PETER 4:8 ESV

Susanna had a hard time forgiving her husband after he blew his whole paycheck on a weekend at the lake with his guy friends. It took days before she could speak to him without anger rising up and weeks to truly get over the pain of what he'd done, especially considering their tight financial state.

Grieved over the pain he had caused, her husband took on extra hours at work to make up for the money he'd blown. Within weeks they were back on top again and the incident was behind them. Susanna operated under the "sadder but wiser" rule and her husband kept his proverbial tail tucked between his legs until he was sure she had truly forgiven him.

Couples bicker over things like this all the time, especially when money is involved. Sometimes when trust is lost, hope follows. But in every case, love can lead the way toward reconciliation. No matter how badly you've been betrayed, you can still pray for love to do its work.

*Lord, I will stand in faith and wait with hope, even in the
hard situations, for Your love to shine through. Love will do
its work and hope will be restored in Jesus' name. Amen. —JT*

Love, the Great Binder

And above all these put on love, which binds
everything together in perfect harmony.
COLOSSIANS 3:14 ESV

If you've ever made a grilled ham and cheese sandwich, you know that putting cheese on both sides of the ham is the only real way to get it to stick to both slices of bread. Cheese is an effective binder when melted. It's terrific in mac and cheese, turning individual pieces of pasta into a cohesive dish. And you'll find it as a topper on things like lasagna because it works to make the whole dish into one cheesy wonderland.

Life is messy. It's made up of different parts. Even within your own home you have different personalities, unique problems, and household woes specific to where you live. Stretch that idea out a bit further—to your neighborhood, your city, or your state—and it's easy to see how overwhelming all of those individual components can be.

That's why we need love. The love of Christ binds us all together like nothing else can. It's the great hope giver for the hopeless, the best remedy for broken relationships, and the easiest formula for mending proverbial fences.

Love. It's like cheese. . .only not as gooey.

Lord, thank You for pouring Your love into our hearts.
It really is the perfect binder. Amen. —JT

False Hope

The way of fools seems right to them,
but the wise listen to advice.
PROVERBS 12:15 NIV

Have you ever been disillusioned? Maybe you put your hope or your trust in someone and they let you down in a big way. Maybe you trusted a politician or an institution, only to learn of corruption at the deepest level. People will let you down. Kingdoms will crumble. If you place your hope in anything other than God, you will surely be disappointed time and time again.

Pause to think about your life for a moment. Are there any "false hope" issues? Have you trusted someone, only to be let down? Have you followed after an ideology or belief, only to find it didn't match the truth of God's Word?

Today is a good day to stop trusting in people and things and place your trust in the only One who won't let you down. There's no such thing as false hope when you're trusting in the Lord alone. He's not going to leave you disillusioned or frustrated. You'll never have to worry about corruption. He's incapable of evil.

Put your trust in Him. He will restore your hope in the best possible way.

Lord, no false hope here! I won't trust in people or things.
I know You won't disappoint me, Father! Amen. —JT

Yesterday Is Past

"Remember not the former things,
nor consider the things of old."
ISAIAH 43:18 ESV

Simon's home was filled with people, all there to see the Savior. Jesus reclined at the table, resting and visiting with those in attendance. Out of the corner of his eye, Simon caught a glimpse of a woman entering the home. A familiar woman. Not the sort to be hanging out at his house, for sure. He started to rise, to send her away, but she approached with something in her hand. What was that? A box. Alabaster. Costly. Maybe she was here to make a donation.

She approached Jesus, who seemed to welcome her with love pouring from His eyes. Simon could hardly believe it when the woman—that ungodly, sinful woman—broke the flask and began to pour priceless oil onto Jesus' head.

The disciples began to argue: "That oil was valuable! It could have been sold and would have fed the poor." But Jesus disagreed. He was happy for the act of worship from the once-sinful woman.

Maybe you can relate. You've come to Jesus broken and sinful. You offer Him your most valuable gift—your life. He accepts it, loves you, and changes your life forever, offering hope like you've never known. Aren't you glad yesterday is behind you?

Thank You, God, for remembering my yesterdays
no more. I'm so grateful. Amen. —JT

This Great Mystery

*To them God chose to make known how great among
the Gentiles are the riches of the glory of this mystery,
which is Christ in you, the hope of glory.*

Colossians 1:27 esv

Melissa couldn't figure out why sorrow and joy seemed to walk hand in hand in her life. She lost her job the same day her boyfriend proposed. The birth of her daughter happened just days after the death of her father. The purchase of her first home came on the heels of a catastrophic illness. Why did the good ride alongside the bad, so close they almost overlapped?

Maybe you've wondered the same thing. You've celebrated great victories just moments after agonizing great losses. You've felt the sting of rejection just moments after witnessing an amazing triumph. It seems so confusing, doesn't it?

The good does walk alongside the bad, and it serves as a reminder. This is part of the great mystery of life—that Christ in you, the hope of glory, will make Himself known in all of it, the good and the bad. You are becoming more and more like Him—in the glory of His resurrection and the fellowship of His suffering.

*You've made Yourself known in my life, Father, in the
agonizing moments and in the blissful ones as well.
Somehow You've restored my hope through it all. Amen. —JT*

Fear, Be Gone!

They will have no fear of bad news;
*their hearts are steadfast, trusting in the L*ORD.
PSALM 112:7 NIV

Sharon was known to all of her friends as the bubbly one. She always had a smile on her face and a song in her heart. If you asked her, even as a teen, what her future looked like, she would always respond, "Wonderful!" She envisioned only great things for herself.

She married in her early twenties, and her husband, who was in the military, was sent to Iraq a short while later. There he faced a life-threatening injury that left him without the use of his legs. When Larry returned to the States, Sharon tried to keep up her optimism. She was cheerful and positive in his presence, but she struggled when she was alone. What would their life be like now? How would they raise their children? This once-bubbly woman nearly crumbled when life's circumstances got the better of her. Fear took hold and she fought to push past it.

Maybe you've been hard hit by fear too. It threatens to steal your hope. Remember, God is in the restoration business. No matter what you're facing, your heart can remain steadfast if you place your hope in Him, not your circumstances.

I'll trust in You alone, God! My hope is in You,
not in what I see around me. Amen. —JT

Hope, a Steadfast Anchor

We have this as a sure and steadfast anchor of the soul,
a hope that enters into the inner place behind the curtain.
HEBREWS 6:19 ESV

Darla wasn't a fan of deep-sea fishing, so when her husband suggested the outing, she balked at the idea. Unable to see past the gleam in his eye, she finally relented. Things went well. . .at first. They boarded the boat and the captain steered them several miles out into the deep, where the better fish would be found.

About ten minutes into the trip, Darla started feeling nauseous. Her stomach threatened to rebel. Thankfully, the boat slowed, the anchor was dropped, and the feelings of seasickness passed. Darla was able to enjoy herself, fishing pole in hand.

Sometimes life gets rocky like that. You're tossed in every direction. You lose your bearings and your hope slips into the murky waters. Then Jesus—your Anchor—steadies the boat. The feelings of sickness pass and you can see more clearly. Your hope is restored once again as He calms your soul.

Father, I've been through some tough seasons. I've been
so out of sorts that I couldn't find my way. But then You
showed up, my Anchor! You settled things down in a hurry
and restored my hope. How blessed I am! Amen. —JT

Growing Stronger

*For whatever was written in former days was written for
our instruction, that through endurance and through the
encouragement of the Scriptures we might have hope.*
ROMANS 15:4 ESV

Jan decided to join a local gym. She wasn't really sure about her goals when she began, but knew she needed to strengthen her upper body so that she could better care for her aging mother. At first, it all seemed impossible. She could barely lift the weights or operate the simplest of machines. And she always seemed to wake up the morning after a workout in so much pain. Staying home was a temptation, but paying that bill to the gym every month served as a motivator. She would keep on trying.

Over a period of weeks, Jan felt herself growing stronger. After six months of steady workout, Jan noticed she was doing longer, harder, more rigorous workouts.

The same is true of your spiritual walk. You start out a weakling. But the more time you spend in the Word, the more those spiritual muscles grow. Your faith is increased, and your hope grows as a result. Keep on working out, girl! You're getting stronger every day.

---

*Lord, I want to grow stronger in You. I won't be a
weakling! I'll keep working out my spiritual muscles
so that I can be a powerhouse. Amen. —JT*

Assurance of Things Hoped For

Now faith is the assurance of things hoped for,
the conviction of things not seen.

HEBREWS 11:1 ESV

Sarah gave her heart to Jesus as a teen and never looked back. With passion leading the way, she became the leader in her youth group. When she graduated from high school, Bible college seemed the right route. Sarah felt an intense calling. She knew that God had big things planned for her life and felt strongly that He was going to use her for His glory.

When she met Mr. Right, Sarah knew she'd found a partner for life. They married, bought a house, and had two children. Sarah never lost her passion for God but sometimes wondered if He'd forgotten to give her the big "calling" she'd dreamed of as a child.

Her youngest—a little girl named Penny—was diagnosed with a neuromuscular disease as a toddler. Sarah turned her attention to becoming an advocate for her child. Before long, others looked to her as an advocate for their children with this illness as well. Within a matter of years, Sarah was running a nonprofit for children just like her little girl.

Did God fulfill His calling? Sure He did. And though it didn't play out as she might have imagined, the outcome was even better.

Lord, I can trust Your plans for my life,
so I won't argue when the picture looks
different than I thought it would. Amen. —JT

Dwell in a Hopeful Land

Trust in the LORD and do good;
dwell in the land and enjoy safe pasture.
PSALM 37:3 NIV

Hannah had a big decision ahead of her. She'd been approved for a mortgage up to a certain amount. There were two houses in her price range that she liked. One was much smaller, but was in a gated community with a lot of trees and parks. The other was more spacious—an older model flip—but happened to be in a rough neighborhood known for break-ins.

In the end, Hannah chose the smaller home in the nicer neighborhood. She was willing to sacrifice space for safety. She wanted to dwell in peace, without having to worry about someone breaking into her house.

God longs for us to dwell in a hopeful, safe place. That's why He keeps calling out to us to abide with Him. When we stick close, we won't have to worry about the enemy's attacks. We can dwell with God and "enjoy safe pasture," as this verse says. It might not look like you envisioned, but in many ways it will be better.

What about you? Are you dwelling in a safe, hopeful place with God? If so, relax and enjoy the freedom His presence brings.

Lord, I'm so glad I get to do life with You.
I will dwell with You all the days of my life,
and for all eternity! Amen. —JT

We Have the Victory

"For the LORD your God is he who goes with you to fight for you against your enemies, to give you the victory."

DEUTERONOMY 20:4 ESV

The world says, "Put your trust and your hope in yourself. Look deep inside to find the answers." But is that good advice? Are answers found within?

Think of the story of Joshua. He stood outside the walled city of Jericho, wondering if he would ever win the battle and take the city. What if Joshua had said to the Israelites, "Put your trust in me, fellas. I've got this! I'm a pretty amazing guy, after all!" Would those walls have fallen?

Of course not! The only way battles are won is by putting our hope in the Lord, not in ourselves or others.

Do you have walls in your life that need to come down? If so, don't turn to self-improvement books (though those may have their place). Don't trust in people. If you're really up against a walled city, put your hope in God. He can, with one breath, knock every wall down.

Sure, work on improving yourself. But let the Lord take the reins and watch the *self*-improvement become *God*-improvement!

I won't trust myself, Father. I'll put my hope in You alone. My battles will be won when I step back and give You control. Amen. —JT

I Won't Be Put to Shame

As we pray to our God and Father about you, we think of your faithful work, your loving deeds, and the enduring hope you have because of our Lord Jesus Christ.

1 THESSALONIANS 1:3 NLT

Enduring hope will not be put to shame. Think about that for a moment. How many times in your life have you been shamed—either publicly or in a small circle of friends? It's hard at any age. To be put to shame is a horrible thing, especially with onlookers wagging their tongues or hyperfocusing on your flaws. Talk about embarrassing!

Your hope in Christ will never be put to shame. Doesn't that make you happy? It will never be proven wrong. That's not to say you'll get what you want when you want it. Sometimes God responds with a no. Other times the miracles take awhile to show up. But you'll never have to wonder if God will fail you. It's simply impossible. He won't put your hope to shame because He's incapable of letting you down. What a wonderful, loving heavenly Father!

Lord, I won't be put to shame for the hope I have in You! I'm so grateful for Your faithfulness. The world tries to put me down, but You never will. How I love You! Amen. —JT

153

Troubling the Teacher

While he was still speaking to her, messengers arrived from the home of Jairus, the leader of the synagogue. They told him, "Your daughter is dead. There's no use troubling the Teacher now."

MARK 5:35 NLT

Jairus could barely catch his breath as he ran toward the crowd. Through the mob of people, he finally caught a glimpse of the One they called Jesus. "P–please, Master! You must come at once. It's my daughter! She's very ill."

Jesus nodded. "I will come, of course." But instead of rushing after Jairus, the Savior took His time. He paused to heal someone else. Jairus ran on ahead and was devastated to learn that his precious little girl had already died. He wanted to blame Jesus, to scream, "If only You. . ."

But the love pouring from the Savior's eyes restrained him. "Don't be afraid, Jairus," Jesus said. "Believe in Me."

Hope was restored in an instant, though Jairus wasn't sure why. And then the unimaginable happened. Jesus arrived at Jairus's home and, with one touch, raised that precious little girl from death to life.

Have you ever felt like you were troubling God? He never minds when you run to Him with your worries and concerns. In fact, He loves when you turn to Him first.

Lord, I'm coming to You. I know You're taking care of the whole universe, but I need You, Father! Help me, I pray. Amen. —JT

Where Is Your Hope Planted?

Those who trust in their riches will fall,
but the righteous will thrive like a green leaf.
PROVERBS 11:28 NIV

Imagine you've been given pumpkin seeds to plant. You could feasibly plant them anywhere—in a pot on your back porch, in the yard, in your vegetable garden. You choose the spot with the very best soil, and before long you're harvesting pumpkins.

Did you know that hope is a lot like those seeds? You can plant it anywhere you like. Some people plant their hope in governments. Some drop their hope-seeds in science or worldly knowledge. Still others plant their hopes and dreams in their children or grandchildren.

Where are your hope-seeds right now? Have you found the right spot to plant them? Maybe you're thinking of putting them into your spouse or even the pastor at your church. Perhaps you're thinking that education is the right field to plant them in. Maybe your job looks like the ideal place.

There's really only one field worthy of those seeds, girl. You've got to plant your hope—all of it—in Jesus Christ. When you do, the harvest will be bountiful!

Lord, I get it! You want me to fix my hope in You,
not in anything the world can offer. I'll prosper
when I plant myself in You. Amen. —JT

Meet Him in Worship

*Praise God in his sanctuary; praise him
in his mighty heaven! Praise him for his
mighty works; praise his unequaled greatness!*
PSALM 150:1–2 NLT

You're facing an uphill battle. A tough diagnosis from the doctor has you wound up in knots. You can't seem to stop thinking, thinking, thinking about all the possibilities. You stay up nights trying to figure out how to fix this. On Sunday morning you don't feel like going to church. You'd rather not, thanks all the same. But when a friend texts to say, "Can I sit by you?" you relent. You drive to the church, your stomach still clenched.

Then the worship service begins. The musicians begin to play that song—the one that punches you in the gut every time. Before long you're completely lost in worship, hands extended, heart wide open to whatever God might want to do. He begins to whisper words of comfort, peace, and hope. Soon those knots in your belly have unwound themselves and are long gone.

God can bring hope through your very act of worship. No doubt you've experienced it time and again. So bring those troubles into your worship time. Watch Him dissolve them, one by one.

*Thank You for meeting me in worship, Lord! I love
to spend my time fully focused on You. Amen. —JT*

It's Not Your Doing

For by grace you have been saved through faith.
And this is not your own doing; it is the gift of God.
EPHESIANS 2:8 ESV

When Jana prayed to receive Christ as Savior at age eleven, her young heart was instantly changed. The pastor of the church baptized her in water the following week and she truly felt like a new creation.

Only one problem—Jana looked to herself to stay holy and clean. When her Sunday school teacher explained that having your sins washed away was like having a chalkboard wiped clean, Jana panicked. How could she keep her chalkboard clean. . .forever? She would have to try really hard not to mess up.

The first time she lost her temper, Jana felt defeated. She could almost see the mark going back up on her chalkboard. And when she argued with her mom the next day, she envisioned another mark. Before long, she was back to where she started. . .or so she thought.

It took a patient mom to explain that Christ's work on the cross covered all of Jana's sins—yesterday, today, and forever. Jana finally learned to trust in the Savior's complete work on the cross and stopped trying to work her way to salvation.

Lord, I'll never be perfect, but You are. I place my
hope in You, my Savior. You took my sins away,
once and for all, and I'm so grateful! Amen. —JT

Pour Out Your Heart

*Trust in him at all times, you people; pour out
your hearts to him, for God is our refuge.*

PSALM 62:8 NIV

Margaret just needed a listening ear. She'd come to the end of a long, grueling week and needed a friend. When Sheila agreed to meet her, Margaret dumped all the woes of the week onto her good friend, barely pausing for breath. Sheila took it all in stride—and even offered encouragement—but Margaret could tell she'd overwhelmed her with the information dump.

Maybe you've been there. You've unloaded all your woes onto an unsuspecting friend. Or maybe you've been that friend on the receiving end. You sat in wide-eyed silence as your BFF downloaded her troubles onto your shoulders.

It's wonderful to be able to pour out your heart, but only God has big enough shoulders to handle it all. So share as you need with those in your circle, but do your best not to overwhelm them. If you do, they might start canceling on your lunch dates! Talk to God. He'll always show up when you need Him.

*Lord, I'm so grateful for friends who listen. Being able to pour
out my woes can be incredibly helpful. But I can tell when I've
crossed a line. I want to be careful not to overwhelm anyone.
I don't ever want to forget that I can always run to You,
Father. You're the best listener ever! Amen. —JT*

Praise Is a Hope Giver

*Through him then let us continually offer
up a sacrifice of praise to God, that is,
the fruit of lips that acknowledge his name.*
HEBREWS 13:15 ESV

Cheery Cherri. That's what people called her. As a child she always had a smile on her face and a song on her lips. She would greet people with a broad grin and jubilant words. That didn't change as she became a teen. People didn't always understand her robust approach to life, but it worked for Cherri.

As a young mom, Cherri began to face some unusual medical issues. She found herself in pain. . .a lot. A diagnosis of rheumatoid arthritis left her curled up on the sofa many days, tears flowing from the pain of her situation.

Somehow, in the midst of it all, her joy remained intact. Pain or no pain, she wasn't going to let the illness rob her of her joy or hope. She continued to praise the Lord, even on the hardest days when she could barely move.

If you've suffered with chronic pain, you know how quickly depression can set in. It might sound cliché to say, "Praise your way through it," but praise really is a hope giver. Don't give up. The Lord will meet you, even in the middle of your pain.

---

*I won't just power through, Lord.
I'll praise my way through! Amen. —JT*

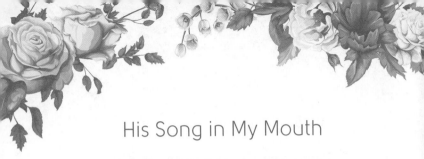

His Song in My Mouth

*He put a new song in my mouth, a hymn
of praise to our God. Many will see and
fear the L*ORD *and put their trust in him.*

PSALM 40:3 NIV

Have you ever known anyone who loved to sing? Maybe your sister would walk through the house singing a song she'd just heard on the radio or hum a familiar tune while driving the car. You could count on her to lead the "Happy Birthday" song at every party, and you weren't surprised when she got the big solo in the church's Christmas production.

People who have music in their souls are fascinating to observe. Even in crisis, they turn to music for comfort and healing. That desire for melody and lyrics is God-breathed. As Psalm 40:3 explains, the Lord put a new song in our mouths, a hymn of praise to Him. Some are more vocal with their song than others, but that's okay! Let the melody He placed in your heart do its work, whether the season you're going through is rough or pleasant. That God-breathed tune will bring hope to your situation and buoy your courage when you need it most.

*Lord, thank You for the song You've placed in my heart. May I
never take it for granted. It's Your gift to me, one meant to lift
my spirits and bring hope. Praise You, Father! Amen. —JT*

The Life Path

Now you've got my feet on the life path,
all radiant from the shining of your face.
Ever since you took my hand, I'm on the right way.
PSALM 16:11 MSG

Remember those mazes you used to work as a kid? You'd take your pencil and start at the beginning then turn it this way and that as you tried to work your way through the maze to the bottom. It was tricky (and sometimes you veered off the right path), but you learned to maneuver through them and even enjoy the challenge.

Some would say that life is like that maze because of its many twists and turns. At times it's difficult to know which way to go. But God knows exactly where you are and where you're headed. You can trust Him to guide you—not all at once, of course, but as you move in faith, step by step. He holds your hand. And, as this scripture says, you're on the right way.

Lord, thank You for laying out a path for me. I can trust
You to guide me every step of the way. I don't have to
be afraid when I can't see around the next corner. You
already know which way I should turn, and You'll let
me know at just the right moment. Amen. —JT

Don't Give Up

I put no trust in my bow,
my sword does not bring me victory.

<small>PSALM 44:6 NIV</small>

It's easy to tell when people have given up. Many times they stop taking care of themselves. Some even stop taking care of their homes or cars. They're so overwhelmed by life that even the smallest chore seems huge.

Maybe you've been there. Your hope is gone and so is your strength. You don't have the energy to do the things you used to. Grabbing lunch with a group of friends sounds exhausting. You use the excuse of laundry, but it doesn't get done either.

It's time to get back in the game, girl! Don't give up for long. There's a great journey ahead, filled with hope and joy. Don't miss it because you're still in your PJs binge-watching TV.

Finding your way back will take energy. And remember, you won't find your victory in anything you can do, but rather through what Christ can do in and through you. He'll give you all you need to get going again. But first. . .stand up! There. Doesn't that feel good?

Lord, I've been lethargic at times. I've felt like giving up.
I've been overwhelmed. I've watched my hope fizzle out. But You
have big things ahead for me, Father, and I refuse to miss them.
It's going to be hard, but I'm standing up, Lord! Amen. —JT

Complete Access

*"And that's not all. You will have complete and free access to
God's kingdom, keys to open any and every door: no more
barriers between heaven and earth, earth and heaven. A yes
on earth is yes in heaven. A no on earth is no in heaven."*
MATTHEW 16:19 MSG

Imagine the Old Testament Levitical priest, dressed in priestly attire, entering the Holy of Holies once a year to offer sacrifices for the people. How his knees must have knocked as he entered into that holy place! How his hands must have trembled. Even one slipup and his story might end right here—in the presence of a holy God.

Aren't you glad we no longer have to go through such challenging circumstances to connect with God? When Jesus died, the veil in the temple tore in two and we now have complete access to the Father. We're like those priests, in that we can connect one-on-one with our Creator, but without the knocking knees and trembling hands.

Complete access! That's what He has given us. Access to His love, His mercy, and His many blessings.

---

*Thank You, Lord, for access into the Holy of Holies.
When I come into Your presence, my hope is
restored and fear has to go. Amen. —JT*

Reconciled

*Together as one body, Christ reconciled both groups
to God by means of his death on the cross, and our
hostility toward each other was put to death.*
EPHESIANS 2:16 NLT

Shari's falling-out with her daughter didn't seem to be a huge deal at first. But when they still weren't speaking nine months later, she began to wonder if they would ever reconcile. Relationships, once severed, are hard to piece back together, and her daughter had a bit of a stubborn streak, to boot. Perhaps she did too.

It took a penitent heart and a lot of humility on both sides, but mother and daughter finally came back together. Before long, they were as close as ever, perhaps even more so. The experience, in some strange way, had bonded them.

Maybe you've been through a schism in a relationship. The cut runs deep and you're pretty sure the damage is irreparable, so you give up hope.

God wants to restore your hope today. Sure, there will be toxic friendships you need to back away from, but most broken relationships can be restored. And here's some really good news: your heavenly Father is also really good at reconciling you back to Him if you've wandered away. Nothing is too big for our awesome God.

*Thank You for reconciling my relationships,
Father. I'm so grateful. Amen. —JT*

God Works behind the Scenes

Yet God my King is from of old,
working salvation in the midst of the earth.
PSALM 74:12 ESV

God never sleeps. Let that sink in for a moment. The average person spends twenty-six years of their life sleeping. Whoa. That's 9,490 days spent sound asleep. But not God! He never sleeps or slumbers. While you're snoozing the hours away, He's taking care of people—and situations—all over the world.

Even when you're awake, you're often not aware of all that God is doing. Even when you can't see it, God is working. Even when you don't feel it, He's on the job. He never ever stops, not even for a moment.

That's where the hope is! When you have hope that God is working behind the scenes on your problem or situation, joy sets in. Hope takes over when you realize He has a plan in motion.

He does, you know. He has a plan in motion even now. And the wheels are already spinning to work things out for your good. What a loving heavenly Father He is!

Lord, You're always working behind the scenes, and that brings
me tremendous comfort. I can't quite figure out how You get
by with no sleep, but I'm grateful to know You're working on
my behalf, even now. Thank You, Father! Amen. —JT

Promises to Claim

*For all of God's promises have been fulfilled in Christ with
a resounding "Yes!" And through Christ, our "Amen"
(which means "Yes") ascends to God for his glory.*
2 CORINTHIANS 1:20 NLT

If you've ever been on the letdown end of a broken promise, you know how painful it can be. It really stinks to put your trust in someone only to have them pull the rug out from under you. Sometimes the incident causes you to withdraw from others or to discount other people's promises as well.

Here's a fun truth: God will never go back on a promise. You can count on Him to fulfill every one. So when He says, "I will never leave you nor forsake you" (Hebrews 13:5 ESV), He really means it. When He promised (in the scripture above) that He would go before you, you can count on it.

You can claim God's promises over your life. Make a list of several promises you find in the Bible. Write them out on sticky notes and fasten them to your bathroom mirror. Study them when you're brushing your teeth or curling your hair. Before long you'll have those promises memorized. They'll come in very handy when you're facing that next big challenge! His promises are "Yes!" through Christ, our "Amen."

*Your promises are yes and amen, Lord! You won't
go back on Your word. I will watch in awe as Your
promises are fulfilled, Father. Amen. —JT*

When Others Fail You

"And whenever you stand praying, forgive, if you have anything against anyone, so that your Father also who is in heaven may forgive you your trespasses."
MARK 11:25 ESV

Amy put her trust in her best friend, Rachel. She shared, in strictest confidence, about her troubled marriage. It never entered her mind that the one she had trusted would betray her by spreading the story, but that's exactly what happened. Before long, Amy was getting text messages and phone calls from concerned friends and family members who wanted more details. She felt sick inside. Why had Rachel done this?

When confronted, Rachel looked shocked to have been caught. "I only told one person," she exclaimed, "and she promised to keep it a secret. I can't believe someone would betray me like that!"

Ugh. Maybe you've been in Amy's shoes. You've been betrayed by a friend. Or maybe you've been part of the gossip train, taking the rumor to the next available set of ears. We're all vulnerable and capable of spreading stories, but it's heartbreaking to our loved ones when we do. We should be quick to forgive, but not so quick to trust the gossips with our next bit of juicy news.

Lord, I've learned my lesson. I know who I can trust and who I can't. Help me to be a trustworthy friend to those who need me most. I don't want to fail those who truly need me. Amen. —JT

God Thinks about You

How precious are your thoughts about me, O God. They cannot be numbered! I can't even count them; they outnumber the grains of sand! And when I wake up, you are still with me!
PSALM 139:17–18 NLT

Falling in love is a wonderful, romantic thing, isn't it? When you're head over heels for someone, you can't sleep, you can't eat, you can't do anything but think about him and long for the next time you'll see him. You get butterflies in your stomach and lose all sense of what's going on around you.

Did you realize that God is head over heels in love with you? It's true! He can't stop thinking about you. You're on His mind day and night. He cares deeply about what you're going through and wants you to know that you're worthy of His love.

How do you feel knowing you're in God's thoughts? Does that knowledge bring you joy? And how are you handling the news that He thinks you're worthy of love? (Some gals don't feel worthy of anyone's love, especially not God's.) Oh, but you *are* worthy! You're a daughter of the Most High God! No wonder He spends so much time thinking about you!

Lord, I love You! And I know You love me too. I'm amazed to know I'm in Your thoughts. I feel so adored. Thank You for Your vast, immeasurable love for me. Amen. —JT

The Glory of His Appearing

*Waiting for our blessed hope, the appearing of
the glory of our great God and Savior Jesus Christ.*
TITUS 2:13 ESV

Have you ever anticipated someone's arrival? Maybe you waited with great anticipation for your best friend to come back into town after moving away. You circled the date on the calendar and couldn't wait! It was all you could think of. Or maybe you got tickets to see your favorite band in concert. You could hardly wait for the big night. You picked out the outfit you would wear, tried out different hairstyles, and even chose the perfect shoes. (Hey, getting ready is part of the adventure!)

You feel an amazing sense of anticipation when you're waiting for someone you love to show up or when you have special plans. Now imagine the person you're waiting for is Jesus. (His Word says He's coming back for us. Now that's exciting!) Believers wait with great anticipation for the day when they will finally see their Savior face-to-face. What a day that will be!

*Lord, I've anticipated so many things in my life, but the
thing I'm most looking forward to is finally meeting You
face-to-face. I'll get to spend all eternity with You, Jesus,
and I can't wait to get the party started! Amen. —JT*

Gratitude

*Therefore let us be grateful for receiving a kingdom
that cannot be shaken, and thus let us offer to God
acceptable worship, with reverence and awe.*
HEBREWS 12:28 ESV

A lovely dew covered the grass. Claire breathed in the cool morning air as she settled into the chair on the back porch with her Bible in hand. She loved this time of day best. In the stillness of morning she felt things more keenly. Claire found herself thankful for so many things. . . . Her wonderful husband. Her three kids. The little grand-daughter whose blue eyes sparkled with joy.

Right now, in the quiet moments on her back porch, she was struck with an overwhelming sense of gratitude for all God had done in her life. Why He had been so good to her, she could not say. She was far from perfect, after all. But He had lavished her with love and blessings anyway.

Maybe you can relate. You're not perfect, but for some reason your perfect heavenly Father continues to pour out life, blessing, and hope. You don't feel deserving of it, but He offers these gifts anyway, free of charge. He's such a good, good Father.

*Lord, I'm overwhelmed with gratitude today. I've done nothing
to deserve Your love, but You pour it out like water from a faucet.
How can I ever thank You enough, Father? Amen. —JT*

Choose Joy

Therefore, since we have been made right in God's sight by faith, we have peace with God because of what Jesus Christ our Lord has done for us. Because of our faith, Christ has brought us into this place of undeserved privilege where we now stand, and we confidently and joyfully look forward to sharing God's glory.
ROMANS 5:1–2 NLT

Did you realize that the Lord commands us to be joyful? It's true! Joy is a choice. If you choose anything other than joy, you'll lose your hope (and hope is one of the most valuable gifts you can receive).

The Bible says we don't grieve as those who have no hope. This is great news because the world is a pretty hopeless place. Don't believe it? Check out the suicide rate. Take a look at the multiplied thousands of people struggling with depression and anxiety. Follow friends on social media. There's a lot of pain out there, and people are having a hard time expressing joy in the midst of it.

You can be different. You can lead by example. As a believer, you can have joy and hope in the middle of your not-so-great circumstances. When you have a sense of purpose, others will want what you have.

Do they want what you currently have?

Lord, I want others to want what they see in me.
May I never throw away my hope or my joy.
Today I choose joy. I choose You. Amen. —JT

Hope When Falsely Accused

Rejoice in hope, be patient in tribulation, be constant in prayer.
ROMANS 12:12 ESV

Joseph leaned against the wall of the prison cell and contemplated his fate. Potiphar's wife had made shocking advances toward him. When he refused her, she turned the tables and accused him of trying to take advantage of her. Nothing could be further from the truth, but how could he prove it? It was her word against his. Now, here he sat in a prison cell, falsely accused. Hope faded as he considered his bleak future.

Maybe you've been falsely accused too. You're locked in a proverbial cell, unable to think clearly because of the false accusation made against you.

In Joseph's case, God intervened and elevated him to a position of leadership in Egypt, second only to Pharaoh. The Lord will redeem your situation too. The key to making it from the accusation to the elevation is found in this one little word: *hope*.

Rejoice in hope. Be patient in tribulation. Be constant in prayer. It's not easy, especially if people are pointing the finger at you or talking about you behind your back. But just as God elevated Joseph, He will redeem your situation too.

Lord, I won't give up hope while I'm waiting for redemption to come. No matter how badly my name is smeared, I will keep trusting in You. Amen. —JT

Never Abandoned

My father and my mother have forsaken me,
but the LORD will take me in.
PSALM 27:10 ESV

The little pup showed up on Linda's doorstep just before suppertime. She could hear the yapping through the door and opened it to discover a little Chihuahua mix, making his presence known.

"Well hello there." Linda leaned down and placed her hand out to see if the dog would greet her. He seemed gentle enough, so she scooped him into her arms. "No collar? I wonder if you're microchipped."

He wasn't. She took him to a local vet to make sure. Then she put a notice on her neighborhood site where other neighbors responded that they'd seen the little dog out and about with no sign of an owner.

Linda ended up keeping the little pup, whom she named Wishbone. Before long, he was part of the family. He'd gone from the life of an orphan to living in the lap of canine luxury, surrounded by humans who loved him to pieces.

Maybe you can relate to Wishbone. Your heavenly Father found you when you were lost on His doorstep. He took you in, cared for you, fed you, and made you part of the family. Now you're His for the rest of your days.

I'm Yours, Lord! I'll never have to worry about abandonment.
You've replaced my emptiness with joy, my despair with hope,
and my worries with peace. I'm so grateful. Amen. —JT

Look Ahead!

*Brothers and sisters, I do not consider myself yet to
have taken hold of it. But one thing I do: Forgetting
what is behind and straining toward what is ahead,
I press on toward the goal to win the prize for which
God has called me heavenward in Christ Jesus.*
PHILIPPIANS 3:13–14 NIV

Life is a race, but God doesn't expect you to run all of it at once.
First, you do some stretching exercises. Then you run around the
block. Then you increase your distance. You keep doing that until
you build up to a longer stretch. You won't be ready for a marathon
until your body is acclimated.

Millie found this out the hard way. On a whim, she signed up to
run a 3k in her hometown. She'd never really considered herself a
runner but thought, *How hard can it be?* Unlike many of the other
participants, she didn't see the need to prepare for the big day. She
figured she'd tackle it in the moment. Imagine her surprise when the
morning arrived and she petered out at the halfway point.

Don't give up. Keep moving forward. Look toward the goal (the
high calling of Christ Jesus). You won't get it right every time, sure, but
it's critical to stay in the race. Before long, you'll be in tip-top shape.

*Lord, I'll stay the course. I'll continue the race.
I'll keep my eyes on You, the author and
finisher of my faith. Amen. —JT*

This Promise Is True

The Lord is not slow to fulfill his promise as some count slowness, but is patient toward you, not wishing that any should perish, but that all should reach repentance.

2 PETER 3:9 ESV

"I'll get around to it, I promise," Natasha's husband said.

For weeks he'd been promising to fix the broken fence along the back of their property.

"The dog got out again today," she told him. "It has to be done soon or things could end badly."

"Soon," he said. "I promise."

Only, days went by and he never got around to it. Finally, in frustration, she contacted a company to do the repairs. Her husband grumbled for a few minutes but got over it.

Maybe you can relate. Maybe someone made you a promise to do something but was slow in following through. Or maybe you've been the one to let a friend or loved one down by not following through on something. Aren't you glad the Lord follows through? You can count on Him and you can trust His timing to be in your best interest. It should bring you great hope to know that He will do all He has promised to do, and all with you in mind.

Thank You, Lord, that You follow through. You keep Your promises in a timely fashion. I'll be patient as I wait, Father. I praise You for all You've done and continue to do for me. Amen. —JT

Vital Connections

From whom the whole body, joined and held together by every joint with which it is equipped, when each part is working properly, makes the body grow so that it builds itself up in love.

EPHESIANS 4:16 ESV

No doubt you've heard the song "Dem Bones." Those compelling lyrics are probably playing in your head now that you've been reminded.

Your ankle bone connected to your leg bone. Your leg bone connected to your knee bone. Your knee bone connected to your thigh bone.

Everything in your body is fitly joined together. (Can you imagine what life would be like if those joints weren't connected?) God planned every last detail of your anatomy with precision in mind.

The Lord is equally as concerned about the connections you make with other believers. He longs for His body to be united and for everyone to work as one corporate body. When you operate like that, you'll have the support system you need during times of crisis, and you'll also have brothers and sisters to celebrate alongside you when you've got great news.

Fitly joined. That's a wonderful, hopeful way to live.

Lord, thank You for the great care You took in knitting my body together. And thank You that I'm "jointly fitted" with my brothers and sisters in Christ. Together, we are very strong indeed. Amen. —JT

Our Help and Shield

All you Israelites, trust in the LORD—
he is their help and shield.
PSALM 115:9 NIV

God is our help and shield. Think about that phrase. He's the shield that protects us from the fiery darts of the enemy. He is our helper, the One who can accomplish what we cannot. He's everything we need when we're up against the enemy. We wouldn't dare enter into battle without asking Him to join us.

Imagine a warrior headed off to battle without his armor. He wouldn't stand a chance without his defensive gear. Without a shield, a sword, and a headpiece, he would be destroyed by his enemy right away. That's what it's like when we face opposition but don't invite the Lord to participate in our struggle. Injuries are inevitable.

Some people think they don't need God. They say things like, "God is just a crutch for the weak." In many ways, He is a crutch, but He's one we can't live without. It was always in His plan to protect and care for His own, so don't spend time defending the way He loves you. Just trust in Him to guard and protect you when you're in the fight.

Lord, I invite You into my struggles. When the battle rages on,
I want You on my side, defending and protecting me. You're
my sword and shield. You're the One who cares most. Thank
You for caring so much about me, Father. Amen. —JT

His Unfailing Love

But I trust in your unfailing love;
my heart rejoices in your salvation.

PSALM 13:5 NIV

"Do you still love me?" Olivia asked her fiancé.

He glanced her way, clearly dumbfounded. "Of course I do. What would make you think otherwise?"

"Oh, nothing. It's just that you haven't said it for a while. I was wondering."

"I love you, Olivia," he responded. "And I always will. You'll never have to doubt it, I promise."

But as the years rolled forward, long after they were married with children, she still had niggling doubts. Many times, she would ask the "Do you love me?" question, only to get the same confused look from him and the same words in response. Why she had those nagging doubts, she couldn't say. He always treated her in a loving manner, after all.

Maybe you're like Olivia. You question whether you are lovable. You can't imagine anyone would love you for long, not with all your flaws.

God will love you forever. He won't change His mind and decide you're not worthy of His love. You're His daughter and He adores you. Get used to hearing "I love you!"

You love me, Lord, and I'll never even have to ask.
That love brings me such hope and joy! Amen. —JT

There's Something about That Name

To them God chose to make known how great among the Gentiles are the riches of the glory of this mystery, which is Christ in you, the hope of glory.

COLOSSIANS 1:27 ESV

Jesus. There's something about that holy, precious name that stirs the heart. The name of Jesus brings comfort when you're hurting, joy when you're wounded, and courage when you're facing obstacles. It conquers foes, lifts spirits, and tells the world where you stand with your faith. When you speak the name of Jesus, you're ready to do business! Nothing can stand in your way.

Take a closer look at this verse: "To them God chose to make known how great among the Gentiles are the riches of the glory of this mystery, which is Christ in you, the hope of glory."

Christ is *in* us. He dwells in the interior catacombs of our heart and takes His rightful place as Creator. He provides the very oxygen we need to survive. And we are in Him as well. To dwell inside the safety of His tent is a privilege and joy.

Christ in you, the hope of glory. What magnificent words. He dwells inside of the believer, bringing unimaginable hope.

Thank You for that powerful name. . .Jesus!
Oh, what a marvelous name it is! Amen. —JT

The Trees Sing for Joy!

*Let the heavens be glad, and let the earth rejoice; let the
sea roar, and all that fills it; let the field exult, and everything
in it! Then shall all the trees of the forest sing for joy.*
PSALM 96:11–12 ESV

The wind whistled through the trees, creating a magical, musical sound. Frances glanced up and saw the golden leaves of the maple tree cascading downward toward the ground. Autumn was fully upon them now.

She spread her arms and turned in a circle, leaves now landing on her face, on her shoulders, and in her hair. Frances felt like a child once again, silly and carefree, at one with nature.

Perhaps you've heard the sound of the wind in the leaves too. Psalm 96 tells us that the trees in the forest sing for joy. Their song isn't written down on a page. Instead, it's played from the heart as the wind whistles through the trees. All of nature praises its Creator. How thankful this marvelous planet is for the One who breathed life into all things.

*Lord, I'm so grateful for nature's glorious song. The ocean
waves, snowcapped mountains, and sandy beaches all
join in the majestic chorus. You are so creative. When I see
the way flowers open in the springtime, I'm filled with
hope. If You can breathe new life into Your creation,
think what You can (and will) do in me! Amen. —JT*

Refuge

It is better to take refuge in the
LORD than to trust in humans.
PSALM 118:8 NIV

"You can trust me."

How many times has someone spoken those words to you in your lifetime? No doubt you've heard them from a boyfriend (who may or may not have been trustworthy). Perhaps you heard those words from a best friend, only to find out later that she was talking about you behind your back. People mean well, but they're fickle. They break their word as easily as they give it sometimes. (Sad, right?)

Many times in your life, you've been asked to place your trust in people—your boss, your spouse, your children, those in leadership over you. Things can get tricky, especially in the workplace, where motives come into question. But ultimately, your trust must be placed in God. When you're wondering if anyone is trustworthy anymore. . .He is. When you're trying to figure out who you can run to. . .the answer is "to the Lord." Take refuge in Him. You're protected there. You can trust Him for the best possible outcome.

Lord, You are my refuge. You're the One I run to when I feel lost
and alone. You cover my sins, but You also cover my heart when
it's broken. Thank You for being my safe place, Father. Amen. —JT

Hope for Broken Friendships

*Instead, you must worship Christ as Lord
of your life. And if someone asks about your
hope as a believer, always be ready to explain it.*
1 PETER 3:15 NLT

Kennedy paced the living room, phone in hand. How could the friendship come to an end so abruptly? She and Lila had been besties since childhood. Now, several twists and turns had led to a dead end. The relationship was over and there was nothing she could do about it, short of praying.

Months went by, but Kennedy never stopped praying. She reached out by text on Lila's birthday, sending a simple, "Happy birthday. Miss you." The word "Thanks" was all she got in response.

It took time, but Kennedy kept chipping away at it. Before long, "I'm sorrys" were spoken, followed by, "Can you forgive me?"

They agreed to meet at a local coffee shop, where both women had a chance to make things right. The words were spoken through tears, but they were spoken nonetheless.

If you've been through reconciliation after a broken friendship, you know the whole thing can be gut-wrenching. Not every friendship is meant to be mended, but when hope for reconciliation is firmly planted in your heart, anything is possible. God is the mender of broken things, the restorer of hope. . .even when restoration seems impossible.

*Lord, thank You for restoring broken relationships. I'm so glad
You're a God who puts things back together. Amen. —JT*

The Free Gift of God

*For the wages of sin is death, but the gift
of God is eternal life in Christ Jesus our Lord.*
ROMANS 6:23 NIV

"Come to our office for this sales pitch, and you will be given a free trip to Cozumel!"

Janet read the advertisement again, not quite believing her eyes. "All I have to do is listen to a sales presentation and they'll give me a free trip?" She made an appointment and went in to listen to the pitch for the time-share property. Janet knew the price of the time-share was out of her range, but she couldn't seem to stop the salesman from his pitch. He just kept going and going, despite her many attempts to stop him.

In the end, there was no free trip to Cozumel. In fact, the only trip she took was back to her apartment, where she soaked in a hot tub and contemplated the agonizing events of the day. She'd been duped and she felt really foolish.

Maybe you've been duped a time or two. It happens, especially in sales. But here's some good news: you'll never be duped by God. It's not in His character to deceive anyone. So rest easy! Keep your hopes high. He will never let you down.

---

*Lord, Your gift of salvation is completely free. It costs me nothing.
You're not trying to con me. You're really giving me Your riches at
Christ's expense, not my own. I'm so grateful! Amen. —JT*

Stop the Negativity Loop

Open my eyes, that I may behold
wondrous things out of your law.
PSALM 119:18 ESV

Remember the old days, when people played vinyl records on a record player? Every now and again a scratch on the surface would cause the needle to skip. The same word of a song would play over and over again, until the needle was lifted and placed back down in a different place.

Sometimes negative thoughts are like that needle. They just keep playing the same negative thought loops, over and over again like a record that keeps skipping, skipping, skipping.

Negative loops cause us to lose hope. When we lose hope completely, we find ourselves in a place known as despair. There's nothing forward-thinking about despair. The best way to counteract it is to lift the needle and place it someplace else in the song.

Are you stuck in a loop right now? Are negative thought patterns causing your life story to remain stuck? Don't give in to despair. See yourself lifting the needle and moving it forward so that your life story can go on.

Lord, I don't want to be stuck. I don't want to be hopeless. I want to move forward. Today I command despair to go in the mighty name of Jesus. In its place. . .blessed, glorious hope. Amen. —JT

Mindset

Those who are dominated by the sinful nature think about sinful things, but those who are controlled by the Holy Spirit think about things that please the Spirit.
ROMANS 8:5 NLT

Racing thoughts. That's really the only way Dawn could describe what went on in her mind on a daily basis. Her thoughts raced through a hundred different scenarios of what could go wrong. If her teen daughter was late coming home, she'd been killed in an accident. If her elderly mother called at an odd time, it must be bad news.

Dawn couldn't seem to control the onslaught of negative thoughts she battled each day. Then she stumbled across this verse from Romans and decided to ask God to control her thought patterns. She gave her thoughts over to the Lord, asking the Holy Spirit to take control.

Maybe you battle an onslaught of fearful thoughts as well. If you're controlled by fear, you will surely feel the same pressure Dawn felt. But that doesn't have to be the case, at least not for long.

Ask the Holy Spirit to control your mind. If you want a hopeful future, one ruled by faith, not fear, give those negative thought patterns to the Lord. He longs for you to be set free even more than you do.

Lord, I'm tired of having a fearful mindset.
Today I give my fears and my thoughts to You.
Control my mind, I pray. Amen. —JT

185

Hope for a Lost World

They are darkened in their understanding,
alienated from the life of God because of the
ignorance that is in them, due to their hardness of heart.

Ephesians 4:18 esv

Elisabeth Elliot waited for news from her husband. He and several other missionaries had boarded their small plane to head to a remote region where the Auca tribe lived. Their mission was top secret and extremely dangerous. When she heard a short time later that all of the men had been killed, Elisabeth fought the temptation to give up on her calling. But her husband, Jim, had been passionate about the tribal people, and she would carry on in his name.

Reaching the world for Christ isn't easy, particularly when you're faced with hostility. And while you might never come up against a crowd of bloodthirsty natives, you do face people every day who are hostile to the Gospel message. It can get overwhelming at times, and you may be tempted to give up any hope of making a difference.

Don't give up. Keep praying. Keep reaching out. If you shine your light in this dark world, you will make a difference for all eternity.

Lord, I get overwhelmed thinking of how lost the people in my world are. I want to shine my light, but it's hard. Give me courage and strength, and don't let my hope wane, Father. Amen. —JT

Hoping in God, Not Hope

"And now, O Lord, for what do I wait?
My hope is in you."
PSALM 39:7 ESV

Have you ever heard the old expression "She's in love with the idea of being in love?" Some people are infatuated with infatuation, for sure! They just can't seem to see past it to reality.

The same could be said of hope. Some people get all hyped up when they're anticipating something. They place their hope in hope, not in the God of hope. This is especially true of children just before Christmas or a birthday. Oh, the anticipation!

It's time to place your hope in something more than excitement or frenzy. Sure, it's fun to get hyped up, but don't let the hype replace the rock-solid faith you need to have in Jesus Christ.

Wait on Him. Trust in Him. Put your hope in Him. You might not work yourself into a lather, but the chances of a true happily-ever-after are much stronger with the Creator of the universe on your side.

I place all my hope in You, Lord, not in hype. (Hoping in hype
is highly overrated! It only lasts so long, then fizzles out.)
You are permanent, stable. You're not going anywhere.
So I'll stick with You, Father. Amen. —JT

That They May Be Saved

*Brothers, my heart's desire and prayer to
God for them is that they may be saved.*

ROMANS 10:1 ESV

Sometimes we forget. It's that simple. Sometimes we forget that one of our primary purposes in life is to share the Good News. We get busy at work. We get preoccupied with complicated relationships. We get burned out, frazzled, and scatterbrained. We don't seem to remember that we have an urgent call on our lives to spread the Good News.

All around us, people are without hope. They've given up. They need to hear the news that Jesus can change their lives—not just for eternity, but for the here and now. Will you be the one to share that news so that hope can be restored and broken hearts mended? It might sound frightening, to step out of your comfort zone, but if you knew that a few moments of discomfort could change someone's life for the better, would you do it?

Be a hope giver. Step out in faith and courage, and share the Good News.

*Lord, I'll admit I've been a little timid when it comes to
witnessing. I've been scared to share the message of what
You've done in my life. I ask for courage, that lives might
be changed and hope restored, Father. Amen. —JT*

Called to Hope

For in this hope we were saved. But hope that is seen is no hope at all. Who hopes for what they already have? But if we hope for what we do not yet have, we wait for it patiently.

ROMANS 8:24–25 NIV

Jacob worked for seven years tending his future father-in-law's flocks to win the hand of his beloved, Rachel. The precious young woman was worth every drop of sweat, every hour of labor. Surely every day Jacob thought about how perfect their union would be.

Unfortunately, he was duped on his wedding day by his boss, Rachel's father. When Jacob lifted the veil of his bride, he found Leah, Rachel's older sister. He was devastated—and imagine how Leah must've felt! Jacob worked another seven years to finally win Rachel's hand. Talk about a journey to get to what you want.

Maybe you've worked long and hard to get where you want to be, only to be disappointed in the end. Perhaps the outcome wasn't at all what you planned and you feel devastated. Don't give up hope. Have the patience of Jacob. Keep working. Keep praying. Keep trying. Surely the end of your story will be worth it if you don't give up.

I won't give up hope, Lord. I'll work harder than ever to see the amazing outcome You'll bring about. Amen. —JT

Salvation Brings Hope

All praise to God, the Father of our Lord Jesus Christ.
It is by his great mercy that we have been born again,
because God raised Jesus Christ from the dead. Now
we live with great expectation, and we have a priceless
inheritance—an inheritance that is kept in heaven for you,
pure and undefiled, beyond the reach of change and decay.

1 PETER 1:3–4 NLT

Do you have friends or loved ones who aren't believers? It's hard, isn't it? Their hopelessness can be hard to watch, especially when you know the answer to their problems. But they simply can't see. . .at least not yet. Those who don't know Jesus Christ as their risen Savior have no hope in this world or the next.

Having an eternal perspective is key to overcoming life's obstacles, which is why nonbelievers struggle. They don't have this perspective. The eternal perspective is vital for anyone who longs to put the past in the past. When you have the hope afforded by an eternal perspective, you know this life's problems are fleeting. You also have the assurance of eternity with the One who created you.

Today, begin to pray in earnest for those who need to know Him. Then live a life that points to Him so that they can be drawn in by His love.

Lord, my loved ones need You. May all I know
and love come to know You, Father. Amen. —JT

Hope for Heaviness

*To grant to those who mourn in Zion—to give them
a beautiful headdress instead of ashes, the oil of gladness
instead of mourning, the garment of praise instead of a
faint spirit; that they may be called oaks of righteousness,
the planting of the LORD, that he may be glorified.*

ISAIAH 61:3 ESV

Shirley worked at her husband's bedside, tending to his every need. Ever since he'd been diagnosed with pancreatic cancer, she hadn't left his side. Sleepless days and nights were taking their toll and she could barely go on. Now, in his final days of life, she could barely stand to see him in so much pain. When he released his final breath, Shirley felt the strangest sense of grief and relief, intermingled. Her heart was broken, but her beloved husband was suffering no more.

Perhaps you've been there. You've watched a loved one grow sicker. You've wondered if God was paying attention. His Word says that He will give the oil of gladness instead of mourning, the garment of praise instead of a faint spirit. It's hard to imagine when the grief is palpable, but He is a God of His word. God will be glorified in the pain of your situation. He will bring beauty from ashes. You can trust Him, even now.

*I won't give up hope, even when I feel faint,
Father. I know when all is said and done,
You will be glorified. Amen. —JT*

Victory through Him

*But thanks be to God, who gives us
the victory through our Lord Jesus Christ.*

1 Corinthians 15:57 esv

"To what do you attribute this great victory?"

Stacey stared into the camera, her eyes filled with tears. She could barely catch her breath after beating out all of her Olympic competitors in the 400m hurdles. Still, the reporter seemed anxious for an answer.

"I. . .I. . ." A lump rose in Stacey's throat. "All of the glory goes to God! Every victory is His!"

The reporter nodded and smiled, then moved on to the silver medalist for her comments.

Maybe you can relate to Stacey's words. Every victory you've celebrated in your life has been from God, after all. While others are taking credit for their achievements, you can't possibly point to yourself. Every achievement is for His glory.

There's no better way to live a faith-filled, hope-driven life than by giving credit where credit is due. What are you thankful for today? What recent victories have left you in a celebratory mood? Be sure to give God the glory for all He's doing in and through you.

*Lord, I praise You for Your goodness in my life. On my own,
I'm nothing. But with You, I am—and have—everything.
I'm victorious in You, Father. Amen. —JT*

Strengthened in the Lord

And David was greatly distressed, for the people spoke of stoning him, because all the people were bitter in soul, each for his sons and daughters. But David strengthened himself in the LORD his God.

1 SAMUEL 30:6 ESV

While King David and his men were away, his enemies, the Amalekites, invaded their land and stole their wives and children. The men were furious with David (as if he had caused this trouble), and he wasn't sure what to do. David went to prayer at once. He asked God, "Do I go after what has been lost?"

God responded, "Go, and I will return what is yours."

That's exactly what happened. David and his men got their families back.

Maybe you've been robbed too. The enemy of your soul has stolen something valuable from you—your child, a friend, a job, perhaps even your home. You never saw it coming and you wonder if the Lord will restore. God is in the restoration business. Trust Him. He's going to make sure you are vindicated and that what was taken from you is returned. Trust Him. Don't give up hope. Call out to Him and be strengthened in the Lord.

Lord, I'm crying out to You. I place my losses at Your feet and ask for restoration, Lord. Please strengthen me and show me what to do, Father. Amen. —JT

Rejoice in the Hope of Glory

*We can rejoice, too, when we run into problems and trials,
for we know that they help us develop endurance. And
endurance develops strength of character, and character
strengthens our confident hope of salvation.*

ROMANS 5:3–4 NLT

Lyn tended to knee-jerk whenever she ran into a problem. Broken dishwasher? The sky was falling. A ding in the car fender? The world was coming to an end. Her extreme reactions made it difficult to take her seriously when tragedy really did strike. People wondered, *Is this another one of Lyn's dramatic reactions, or is it real?*

Believers will go through various trials in this life, but we don't have to lose it when things happen. We certainly don't have to give up hope when faced with a challenge. The Holy Spirit is right here, dwelling inside us, to bring hope and courage.

Are you a knee-jerker? Do people roll their eyes when you begin to carry on about your latest woe? If so, take a deep breath and allow the circumstance to grow you into the woman of God you are meant to be.

*Lord, I'm sorry for the times I overreact. I don't mean to.
It's a learned behavior, for sure—a tough habit to break.
I want to grow in You. Help me, I pray. Amen. —JT*

Count Your Blessings

You will eat the fruit of your labor;
blessings and prosperity will be yours.
PSALM 128:2 NIV

Kristin felt overwhelmed. She could hardly keep up with everything—the kids, the house, her job, the meals she had to cook. It felt impossible at times. Sometimes she couldn't see past all of the struggles and pain to the blessings. She forgot to remember that each of these things—from her kiddos to the laundry—was a gift from God.

What about you? Do you ever forget to count your blessings? Are you ever so caught up in the daily grind that you forget that the cup of coffee in your hand is a gift? So is the car you drive to work. So is that job, of course. And the paycheck that comes with it.

Counting your blessings (vocalizing your thanks for what God has given you) will bolster your faith and increase your hope. When you see what you already have, you're far less likely to complain about the tasks that aren't yet complete or the needs that haven't been met.

Lord, I'll do it today! I'll make my list and check it twice. I'll try to remember all of the many, many ways You're already blessing me, Father. I won't overlook what's right in front of me. Amen. —JT

Hope Reborn

Jesus replied, "Very truly I tell you, no one can see the kingdom of God unless they are born again."
JOHN 3:3 NIV

Perhaps you've been to a funeral of a friend or loved one who didn't know Christ. Everyone shared stories about what a wonderful time the deceased must surely be having in heaven. But you had your doubts. Based on your friend's staunch disbelief in God, how could he be in heaven now?

No one knows how God operates in those final moments of life, of course. Perhaps your friend met Jesus in an amazing eleventh-hour encounter. But one solid truth remains—in order to see heaven, you must be born again. You must have an encounter with the Savior of the World, Jesus Christ.

This world is in a downward spiral, moving away from God. There's no greater time to bring hope to the hopeless than right now, when the odds seem to be stacked against Christianity. Be a light in the darkness. Lead people to Christ. There's no greater joy than knowing your loved one has passed from this life straight into the arms of Jesus.

Lord, I want to do a better job of reaching people for You. Give me courage and strength to bring hope to a hopeless world, Father. Amen. —JT

Spring Has Sprung!

*There is a time for everything, and a season
for every activity under the heavens.*
ECCLESIASTES 3:1 NIV

Geneva backed her car out of the driveway and then shifted into drive. As she did, her neighbor's garden caught her attention. "Wow! Beautiful!" Pink and red azaleas filled the front garden. They seemed to have bloomed overnight. What a difference the color made to the yard. The whole yard seemed alive with color and hope. And what about those gorgeous green leaves suddenly springing to life in the trees along the edge of the highway? They were magnificent!

As Geneva discovered, springtime is filled with possibilities. Opportunities. Adventures. Hope for things yet unseen. Springtime adds color to your life, hope to your soul, and joy to those around you. It's a time of refreshment and excitement, when you're wondering what God is up to and where He will take you next.

Think of the last spiritual springtime you enjoyed. What was God speaking to your heart? Did those things come to pass? If so, what fun you must have had, stepping out in faith. There will be many more seasons like that for you, woman of hope! Great adventures lie ahead.

---

*I love new adventures, Lord. Keep speaking
to my heart. I'm listening! I can't wait to see all
the things You've prepared for me. Amen. —JT*

Walking Alongside the Hopeless

*When the righteous cry for help, the L*ORD* hears and delivers them out of all their troubles. The L*ORD* is near to the brokenhearted and saves the crushed in spirit.*

P SALM 34:17–18 ESV

When Susan's best friend Aggie lost her husband of forty-three years, she did her best to be present. Not a day went by when Susan didn't call Aggie or offer to take her to lunch. The first few weeks she tried to console her friend, but when financial troubles began to plague Aggie, Susan wasn't sure what to do.

Aggie reached a point of hopelessness about a year into her journey as a widow. Her situation wasn't as dire as she made it out to be, but she rehearsed the story time and time again, and always in front of a captive audience.

What about you? Are there people in your circle who are so down—so hopeless—that you find it difficult to hang out with them? If so, how do you cope? Are you able to continue to shine your light, even when you'd rather turn and walk away? God will honor your patience with those who've given up. They need your encouragement and your joy. Continue to bless them, no matter how hard.

Lord, I'll do my best with the tough cases. Thank You for showing me how to love as You love. Amen. —JT

Every Good and Perfect Gift

Whatever is good and perfect is a gift coming down to us from God our Father, who created all the lights in the heavens. He never changes or casts a shifting shadow.
JAMES 1:17 NLT

We are trained from childhood to take credit for the things that go right in our lives. Study hard and you get an A on the test. Work hard on your gymnastic skills and you win the competition. We get to the end of the challenge, accept the prize, and say, "Yes, I did that."

God wants us to hope for the best in all of our endeavors, but He also wants us to remember that every good and perfect gift comes from Him. That wonderful man you fell in love with? He came from God. That job where you work? It's His gift to you. Those friends you adore? They were sent straight from heaven.

Sure, you'll accomplish many things in your life. You really are going places. But don't ever let the pride of your accomplishments nudge out the truth of God's role. He has always been there for you and always will be. And He has plenty more gifts ahead. So hold on for the ride, girl.

Lord, I don't place my hope in myself or my own accomplishments. I place it all in You. Every wonderful thing that has ever happened to me has come from You. Have I mentioned how grateful I am? Amen. —JT

Walk in Wisdom

Those who trust in themselves are fools,
but those who walk in wisdom are kept safe.
PROVERBS 28:26 NIV

Maria was always second-guessing herself. She decided to move into a new apartment, then almost backed out on moving day. She fell head over heels for the man of her dreams, agreed to marry him, and then almost left him at the altar. Thank goodness, common sense took hold at the last minute and she followed through.

Still, her insecurities lingered through the years. No matter what decisions she made in life, she nearly always changed her mind—or thought about changing her mind.

Maybe you can relate to Maria. You second-guess yourself a lot too. One of the reasons people do that is because they know they can't trust their feelings. Human beings are fickle, after all. Perhaps that's why God reminds us in this scripture that we're not supposed to put our trust in ourselves. Our hope is in Him. To walk in wisdom is to give yourself wholeheartedly to the Savior of your soul, to trust in Him implicitly. There will be no second-guessing when you're following His lead, after all.

Lord, thank You for being trustworthy! I will put my
trust in You, not myself. I won't have anything to
second-guess when I stick with You. Amen. —JT

Rooted in Him

*I fall down on my knees and pray. . .that out of his glorious,
unlimited resources he will give you the mighty inner
strengthening of his Holy Spirit. . . . May your roots go down
deep into the soil of God's marvelous love; and may you be
able to feel and understand, as all God's children should,
how long, how wide, how deep, and how high his love really is.*
EPHESIANS 3:15–18 TLB

Randi and her family hunkered down in the living room of their house
as the hurricane roared overhead. She could hear the wind howling
through the trees and felt sure—at least at one point—that she could
also hear trees falling.

When they awoke in the morning, she and her husband decided
to take a peek outside. Randi could hardly believe her eyes when she
saw that a neighbor's massive pine tree had come down.

Hurricanes. Tornadoes. High winds. These things all wreak havoc
on trees. The most vulnerable trees are those whose roots do not run
deep. They topple with little effort. No wonder we lose faith when
we don't plant our roots deep. To maintain our growth, we have to
let those roots go way down. Staying in His Word, praying, spending
time in worship. . .these are all ways to dig deeper.

---

*I want deep roots, Father. I don't want to topple
when the storms of life blow through. Amen. —JT*

Keep Doing Good

And let us not grow weary of doing good,
for in due season we will reap, if we do not give up.

<small>GALATIANS 6:9 ESV</small>

When the Lord told Jonah to go to Nineveh, he balked at the idea. Why preach to such wicked people? He'd rather see them perish. So he took off for Tarshish instead. God caught up with Jonah in the belly of a whale sometime later, and they had what we would call a "come-to-Jesus meeting." Jonah regretted his decision to run from what he should have been doing.

What about you? Have you ever run from God when His instructions seemed too hard? Have you ever panicked and moved in the opposite direction? It's easy to lose hope when the task seems too great, but remember: God won't call you to something unless He plans to equip you for it. In other words, you have nothing to fear.

Keep doing good. . .even when it's hard. You will reap a reward for your faithfulness, if not in this life, then in the life to come, but only if you don't give up.

Lord, I'll admit, there are times I want to hightail it out of here, to run as fast and far away from Your instructions as I can. Following them seems too hard. But I won't quit, Father. I'll keep doing good—for Your glory and the sake of Your kingdom. Amen. —JT

Comforted

"Blessed are those who mourn,
for they will be comforted."
MATTHEW 5:4 NIV

It's been a long day. You faced unexpected challenges that had you tied up in knots. But you're home now, ready to put the stresses of the day behind you. The kids are tucked into bed and you've had a nice hot bath. Now you're in your PJs, ready to climb into bed.

You slip between the covers and settle back with a book. Propped up on the pillows, you reach for the comforter and pull it up, up, up to your chin. There, snuggled in the bed, you're more comfortable than you've been all day. In that moment, all troubles vanish.

Now picture yourself after a long, stressful ordeal. You reach out to the Lord and He invites you to join Him for some quiet time. There, in that precious place, He comforts you in the same way a blanket does. He brings warmth to your soul, hope to your dreams, and joy to your heart.

Do you need to be comforted today? Slow down. Stop stressing over the day. Put it behind you. Draw near to God and watch as He restores your soul.

Lord, I'm grateful for the comfort that only You can bring.
Never let me forget that I can run to You when I feel I
have no place to go. You restore my hope, Father, and I
thank You for a change of perspective. Amen. —JT

Discipline Yourself

For the moment all discipline seems painful rather than pleasant, but later it yields the peaceful fruit of righteousness to those who have been trained by it.
HEBREWS 12:11 ESV

Trina's new puppy had quite a few behavior issues. She decided to train him, but knew it wouldn't be easy. Trina started with basic commands: sit, stay, down, and roll over. When he conquered those, she moved on to bigger things, training him to ring a bell hanging from the doorknob whenever he needed to go outside.

Disciplining a dog is a lot of work, but the payoff is great. Having an obedient, disciplined pup means a less stressful life. The same is true when we discipline ourselves. Taking the time to say, "I'll load that dishwasher right after dinner," or "I'll make my bed in the morning, even though no one is going to see it," is a choice, but it's a good one.

What areas of your life could use more discipline? You'll lead a much happier, healthier life if you dive right in and get those tasks done. You'll feel so much better about yourself and your situation.

Lord, it's easy to become hopeless when life seems out of control. Thank You for the reminder that I can discipline myself to live a healthy life in You. Amen. —JT

When Hardship Goes on Too Long

*There is no fear in love. But perfect love drives
out fear, because fear has to do with punishment.
The one who fears is not made perfect in love.*
1 JOHN 4:18 NIV

Mindy trudged her way through the darkest season of her life. When her husband was diagnosed with ALS, she felt she'd faced the darkest night. But the years after proved her wrong. She felt her faith give way as fear and anger crept in. Sometimes, in the wee hours of the night, she would cry until she was completely depleted.

It's hard enough to go through a rough season, but when that season drags on, things can reach a crisis point. Most of these seasons feel like they will never end, but they always do—sometimes with a happy outcome, other times a tough outcome. How you live out these seasons is critical to your emotional survival.

Don't give up hope. It sounds cliché, but having hope for your future is so important. Don't let your circumstances overwhelm you. Remember, God is in it with you for the long haul. He's never going to leave you, no matter how deep the valley gets.

*Lord, there are times I feel I can't take another step. I can't keep
going. But You sweep in and give me hope for the future. It makes
no sense in the moment to be hopeful, but I'm so grateful when
those moments come. Praise You, Lord. Amen. —JT*

Contentment

Not that I am speaking of being in need, for I have learned in whatever situation I am to be content. I know how to be brought low, and I know how to abound. In any and every circumstance, I have learned the secret of facing plenty and hunger, abundance and need.

PHILIPPIANS 4:11–12 ESV

What does it mean to be content? Have you struggled with discontentment? Consider Maggie's story. Growing up, she felt an undercurrent of discontentment in her heart. When her parents took her on a trip to the lake, she argued that an amusement park would have been more fun. When she got a B+ on a test, she fumed. It should've been an A. Nothing was ever good enough. Every situation left her longing for more. She spent more time grumbling than praising, which often left her friends rolling their eyes.

Maybe you can relate. You struggle with discontentment too. You live in a wonderful house, but it's not as nice as your friend's. You have a great job, but you wish you made more money. The Lord wants you to be content. Being chronically discontent leads to unnecessary hopelessness. You feel cheated.

God has given you everything you need. You're definitely not cheated. You have so much more than many of the people around the world. So turn that discontentment into praise and watch your attitude change!

Lord, I'm content in You. I'll stop whining about what I don't have. Amen. —JT

Anticipation

You make known to me the path of life;
in your presence there is fullness of joy;
at your right hand are pleasures forevermore.
PSALM 16:11 ESV

Sophie could hardly wait to go to church camp. Her mother made a calendar and fastened it with magnets to the refrigerator so that Sophie could mark off the days one by one. She could just imagine all the fun things she would do at camp—swimming in the lake, playing games with her friends, and attending services in the evenings.

When the day arrived, Sophie boarded the church bus with her suitcase packed. She could hardly wait to get on her way.

Maybe you've had that same sense of anticipation about some big event in your life. Maybe you're like a child. . .you never stop hoping and looking forward with great expectation.

Oftentimes, the most joyful part of all is the hoping. Your faith and trust are in the thing you've hoped for, without wavering. Maybe that's why Jesus said to come as a little child. He wants us to come with high expectations and to be joyful in our anticipation.

Lord, I love the sense of joy that comes with anticipation.
I can't stop hoping. . .and I don't want to! Thanks for
making this journey so much fun, Father! Amen. —JT

Curiouser and Curiouser

It is the glory of God to conceal things, but the glory of kings is to search things out. As the heavens for height, and the earth for depth, so the heart of kings is unsearchable.
PROVERBS 25:2–3 ESV

Don't you love watching children at play? They have such intense curiosity, and they're always asking, "What is that?" or "What does that mean?" Kids aren't satisfied with a simple answer. They want details. They marvel at the wind whipping through the trees, the sound of a cricket chirping, and the dew on the grass in the morning. They turn empty boxes into cars or trains and bedsheets into forts. Everything is an adventure to them.

God loves when we come to Him with the curiosity of a child. There's a precious sense of animation and anticipation when we approach Him with childlike wonder.

How is your curiosity level? Is your spiritual journey a childlike adventure, filled with new things to do and learn? It can be! Ask God to give you spiritual eyes to see things the way a child would see them. What fun you will have as you journey forward with God.

---

*Lord, I want to have the joy and curiosity of a child.
No more humdrum for me! I want to anticipate,
to enjoy, and to search things out. You have made
my life an adventure, Father! Amen. —JT*

Reframe Your Experience

We look not to the things that are seen but to the things that are unseen. For the things that are seen are transient, but the things that are unseen are eternal.
2 CORINTHIANS 4:18 ESV

"You just need to look at things differently."

No doubt you've heard these words a time or two. Maybe you've even spoken them. So many of life's situations require reframing, after all.

To reframe an experience means you look at it from a different perspective. The storm that blew your roof off meant you got a new roof and a renovated house. The flight you missed meant you got to stay an extra day with your family before going to a boring work-related conference. The loss of your job gave you the courage to finally follow your dreams and get your real estate license.

Are there situations in your life right now that need reframing? Instead of getting bummed about the bad things, just slant your perspective. Try to see things with a hopeful eye, a positive spin. Don't get bummed. . .get reframed!

Lord, thank You for helping me reframe the tough situations in my life. I want to have the best possible outlook, no matter what I'm facing. I'm so grateful for Your help as I look at things through Your eyes. Amen. —JT

What's the Reason?

But in your hearts honor Christ the Lord as holy,
always being prepared to make a defense to anyone
who asks you for a reason for the hope that is in you;
yet do it with gentleness and respect.

1 PETER 3:15 ESV

"How do you do it?" Janie's friend asked.

"Do what?"

"Stay so upbeat all the time. Why are you always so happy?"

Janie paused to consider her friend's question. "It's not that I'm always happy. I've been through a lot of rough patches. But in every situation God has proven Himself faithful. So I guess you could say I've learned to trust Him. I've learned to put my hope in Him, not the situation."

"I see." Her friend grew quiet. "Whether you know it or not, Janie, I've been watching you, and I want to be more like that. Thank you for showing me it's possible."

Janie couldn't help but smile. She hadn't even realized her friend was watching, so this conversation surprised her. But she thanked God that He had known all along.

People are watching you too. They want to know why you're always so hopeful, so filled with life. Be prepared to give an answer when they ask!

Lord, I'm ready to share the Good News with anyone
who asks. Thank You for the joy inside of me. Amen. —JT

Firstfruits

*Honor the LORD with your wealth and
with the firstfruits of all your produce.*
PROVERBS 3:9 ESV

Tori always worried about money. Whether her bank account was full or empty, she carried a burden in her heart that she might someday have to do without the things she needed. Her worries stemmed from a childhood filled with financial woes. Many times, she'd come home from school to discover that the electricity had been cut off or the water didn't work.

No matter how hard she worked, Tori still felt hopeless about her financial future. It wasn't until she came to an understanding about giving her firstfruits to the Lord that she finally understood God's plan for finances.

Give. . .and it will be given unto you. Give. . .and the Lord will surely give you everything you need. It made no sense at first, but her hope was restored as soon as she began to give. She couldn't help but notice that the Lord made provision for every need, even though she was giving 10 percent away. Tori began to appreciate God's math.

What about you? How do you feel about giving your firstfruits to the Lord? It requires faith, sure, but your hope will grow alongside your trust as you watch your heavenly Father step in and meet every need.

*I trust You, Lord. I'll give generously and watch in
awe as You take care of my needs. Amen. —JT*

Purpose

The LORD will fulfill his purpose for me; your steadfast love,
O LORD, endures forever. Do not forsake the work of your hands.
PSALM 138:8 ESV

Amber felt she didn't have a sense of purpose in her life. She had no driving force. She just meandered from project to project, relationship to relationship. Her jobs felt a bit lifeless. So did her relationship with God. She went through the motions while going to church but didn't really feel the connection she'd once felt with the Creator of the universe.

At a women's retreat Amber finally took the time to dig deep and break free from some of the things that had been holding her back. She recommitted her life to the Lord, to His purposes, His love, His forgiveness. In that moment, all the pretense faded away and a genuine desire to begin again took hold. When that happened, her hope returned in full force.

What about you? Do you feel a sense of purpose driving you? The Lord will fulfill His purpose in you and will sustain you with His love. That's a promise you can take to the bank.

Lord, thank You for giving me a sense of purpose and instilling
a desire for genuineness in my life. I don't want to just go
through the motions—in my life or in my relationship with You.
All I want from this point forth is the real deal. Amen. —JT

Focus

Let your eyes look directly forward,
and your gaze be straight before you.
PROVERBS 4:25 ESV

"Keep your eye on the prize." No doubt you've heard that phrase a time or two. Whether you're trying to win a ball game or ace a test, keeping your focus is critical.

The same is true of your spiritual walk. When you keep your eye on the prize—Jesus—everything else falls into place. If you seek first God's kingdom, everything else will be added to the equation.

The opposite is true as well. If you remove Jesus from His rightful place—the center of your life—everything gets blurry. You lose focus, you lose hope, you lose sight of His plans for your life.

Is Jesus in your line of vision, the center of all you say and do? If so, great! If not, perhaps it's time to refocus and invite Him to be your all in all. Keep your eyes on Him, directly forward, and keep your gaze fixed on the prize, not the superfluous things to your right and left. He is truly everything you could ever hope for or need.

Lord, I'll keep my eyes on You. You're my prize, Jesus.
I won't get distracted by things that tempt me to
look away. You're all I need, Lord. Amen. —JT

Heirs According to Hope

*Because of his grace he made us right
in his sight and gave us confidence
that we will inherit eternal life.*

TITUS 3:7 NLT

There was no doubt in anyone's mind that Tracy would be included in her stepdad's will. He had loved her like his own daughter for over forty years, after all. As she sat in the attorney's office listening to the reading of the will, her emotions swelled. To be included meant she was truly part of the family—blood-related or not.

If you've been through the reading of a loved one's will, you know how precious it is to see those children and grandchildren included. And if you've been the unexpected recipient of someone's generosity, it can be overwhelming. To be included in the family is a special privilege, one you don't take lightly.

God has included you in His family. He has swept you into the fold, added you to the will, and made special provision for you. You'll be spending eternity with Him, in fact. Today, take the time to thank your heavenly Father for His gift of inclusion. What a loving Father He is!

*Lord, I feel such joy knowing that You wanted me as Your child.
What hope I have, knowing that eternity is mine, thanks to
Your provision. Thank You, precious Lord! Amen. —JT*

Leap of Faith

*Trust in the LORD with all your heart; do not depend on
your own understanding. Seek his will in all you do,
and he will show you which path to take.*
PROVERBS 3:5–6 NLT

Deena stood on the edge of the ditch, trying to measure the distance to the other side.

"Don't just stand there," her brother called out. "Jump!"

Her little legs wobbled as she tried to imagine what it would be like if she fell in the murky waters in the ditch. At only ten years old, she didn't have very long legs.

"Don't think about it!" Samuel called out. "Jump, Deena. Jump!"

And so she jumped. Her shoes got wet as she landed just short of the grass on the other side, but she made it. Whew!

Maybe you know what it's like to have to take a leap of faith as well. You have an opportunity to take a new job, but you're scared. You've been given the chance to go on a mission trip to Africa, but you're terrified.

The reason faith-jumps are referred to as leaps of faith is because they require jumping into the unknown. You don't know how—or if— you're going to land. But God knows! And He's big enough to help you across the ditch. So what are you waiting for? Jump, girl! Jump!

---

*Lord, my knees are wobbly, but I'm going to do it.
Here I go! I'm taking a leap of faith! Amen.* —JT

No Shame Here

*And hope does not put us to shame, because God's
love has been poured out into our hearts through
the Holy Spirit, who has been given to us.*
ROMANS 5:5 NIV

Mary and Martha were pretty typical, as sisters go. They were different in personality but shared the same home. When Jesus came for a visit, Martha—the worker bee—got straight to work, playing hostess. She fussed, fussed, fussed, taking care of her house, the food, and her guests. Not Mary. She sat at the feet of Jesus, completely at ease, listening to Him speak and basking in His presence.

Mary's stillness didn't sit well with her sister. Martha fumed that Mary wasn't up working alongside her. But Jesus had a few tough words for Martha: "Mary has chosen what is better" (Luke 10:42 NIV).

Ouch. Those words must have stung. Martha was, after all, the hostess with the mostest. She was making sure Jesus and the other guests were well tended to.

The next time you feel like taking some time off just to rest, to sit at Jesus' feet, don't let guilt convince you that you need to keep going. Hear the words of your Savior as He calls out, "Mary has chosen the better thing."

Spend time with Him. It's what He longs for most of all.

*Lord, I'll pause from my labors and spend time with You.
I won't get so busy that I forget to sit at Your feet. Amen. —JT*

The Challenge of Waiting

But if we hope for what we do not see,
we wait for it with patience.
ROMANS 8:25 ESV

Lila applied for a grant for her new ministry. She waited. . .and waited. . .and waited some more. It felt like ages before she heard back that the grant had been approved.

Maybe you've had to wait on something important too—news about a pending mortgage, test results related to a health diagnosis, or your grades at the school semester's end.

Hope requires endurance. When we don't get what we hope for right away, patience is called for, time is called for. Think of a runner, headed toward the finish line. It's going to be several minutes before the end is in sight, but he keeps running all the same. Endurance comes as a result of waiting. It's a real challenge to wait and hope and not give up, especially if circumstances seem to be against you. But you have the assurance that God will be with you no matter the outcome. You don't have to fear.

Lord, I've never been very good at waiting, but I can see that endurance is being built inside me as I hang on. I can't see the finish line yet, but I know that You are there, waiting for me. That makes the race more bearable. Amen. —JT

A Heroic Resolution

For freedom Christ has set us free; stand firm therefore,
and do not submit again to a yoke of slavery.

GALATIANS 5:1 ESV

If you've ever found yourself in bondage to a particular sin, there's good news for you today! Hope can be restored as you are set free. If you have put your trust in Christ, He brings you a heroic resolution against the lusts that once held you bound. You can be joyfully set free as you trust in Him and His promises.

When hope enters the picture, chains have to fall. When hope comes on the scene, lusts and bondages have to flee. When hope takes over, God's promises are taken to heart. They become more than simply words on a page in the Bible. They're real, living, breathing messages to the reader who takes them to heart.

Today I ask for a restoration of hope, Lord! I want
the chains of bondage to fall off once and for all,
that I might be set free in You. Please provide a heroic
resolution to the challenges of my life, I pray. Amen. —JT

More Inspiration for Your Beautiful Soul

How God Grows a Woman of Faith

How God Grows a Woman of Grace

How God Grows a Woman of Joy

How God Grows a Woman of Prayer

Hardcover / $12.99 each

These delightful books will enhance your spiritual journey as you embrace the inspiration, encouragement, and refreshment offered in each devotional reading.

About the Authors

JANICE THOMPSON, who lives in the Houston area, writes novels, nonfiction, magazine articles, and musical comedies for the stage. The mother of four married daughters, she is quickly adding grandchildren to the family mix.

ANITA HIGMAN, an award-winning author from Texas, enjoys traveling to exotic places, Spanish TV dramas, antiquing, fairy-tale everything, gardening (even though she has no idea what she's doing), all things Jane Austen, making brunch for her friends, and writing.